Save Your Life www.saveyour

Save Your Life

By Philip Raby

Inspired by my parents, Bert and Pauline Raby, who always lived life to the full.

Dedicated to my children, Louisa and Jonny, the next generation of lifesavers.

"The trick is to enjoy life. Don't wish away your days, waiting for better ones ahead."
Marjorie Pay Hinckley

www.saveyourlife.me

Save Your Life www.saveyourlife.me

First published 2017

Copyright © Philip Raby 2017

All rights reserved.

Published by Solid Air Publishing

All rights reserved. No part of this publication may be reproduced in any form without the prior written permission of the author.

All recommendations within this book are made without any guarantee on the part of the author or publisher, who also disclaim any liability incurred in connection with the use of this book.

Note that the stories told in this book are all based on real people but the names and some details have been changed to protect their privacy.

www.saveyourlife.me

Introduction

"Voom! What was that? That was your life, mate. That was quick, do I get another? Sorry mate, that's your lot."
Basil Fawlty

"I hate my job," admits Dave, "but if I stick at it for the next thirty years or so, I'll get a really good pension. I started worked for a big insurance company when I left university, and I've been there ten years already. I'm good at what I do, but I dread Monday mornings, knowing I've got to drag myself into the office for another week. The only thing that keeps me going is the thought of a comfortable retirement at the end of it."

What a depressing thought. Spending the majority of your adult life doing something you don't enjoy just so you can have some money for your final years when, let's face it, you may not be active enough to do all you want to. Indeed, it's possible you may not even be alive at all.

"My father worked hard all his life in banking and built up a fabulous pension pot, then he died of a heart attack at 64, just before he retired," says Elizabeth. "My mum and I were devastated, not just because we'd lost such a wonderful man but also because he'd always talked the things he was going to do 'when he retired'. He had lots of plans, including travelling to South America, walking from England's coast to coast, and going on a cruise. Sadly, it wasn't to be."

Unlucky cases? Maybe; but unfortunately, not uncommon ones. Do you ever chat with people who moan about having to go to work on a Monday morning and say they can't wait for retirement? In fact, there's an excellent chance that you are one of those people, which is why you're reading this book. What's more, spending your life doing a stressful job you don't enjoy will be detrimental to your health and could just lead to an early death (in fact, the Japanese even have a word for this – Karōshi, death from overwork) or, if not, at least poor health in old age. Most people have at least a 40-year working life; that equates to 1920 weeks. 9600 working days or – wait for it – 76,800 hours on the money-making treadmill. That's an awfully long time to spend doing something you don't enjoy, especially when you're only likely to be awake for 233,600 hours in those 40 years.

Life is short, and you only get one stab at it, so surely it makes sense to enjoy every day, not just the ones from age 65 onwards. After all, one of those days will be your last and, thankfully perhaps, most of us don't know when that one will be. There's something inherently wrong with a system whereby we defer living the life we want until we've reached the final years of our existence. Work has become something we do so we can stop doing it – surely there must be a better way.

Author Timothy Ferris, in his excellent book, *The Four Hour Work Week*, suggests having a series of mini-retirements throughout life, which is an inspired idea. However, I suggest taking it one stage further and living an entire life of retirement. How does that grab you?

Impossible? Well, if your idea of retirement is having a lot of disposable income and spending your days lazing about on luxury cruise liners drinking champagne, then maybe it is impossible unless you have built up an extremely fat pension pot.

Let's have a reality check here; if you continue on your present trajectory through life, how good a pension will you end up receiving? In recent years most pension plans haven't performed as well as expected, and people are, on average, living longer than ever, so that means pension funds have to pay out for more years. Years when you'll have plenty of time on your hands to spend money. Assuming, that is, you'll have enough cash for anything more than the basics in life. The fact is, retirement is a dream that people look forward to with rose-tinted spectacles. When you finally arrive at it, you may not have the cash or the health (or even a life, for that matter) to make the most of it.

The alternative dream for many people is to win the lottery next Saturday evening, hand in their notice and live a life of leisure, starting the moment those magic numbers are drawn. There are, though, two inherent problems here. First, it's very unlikely to happen; the lottery isn't called a tax on the stupid for nothing. In the UK, you have a one in 14-million chance of winning (which means, incidentally, that buying several tickets each week is going to have little effect of increasing your chances, so if you do like a flutter, one ticket per draw is enough). Second, assuming you do pick the golden ticket, suddenly receiving an enormous amount of money can mess up your life. No, really; think about it for a moment – if you never had to work again, what would you do with your life? Seriously, once you've bought the big house, the flash cars, been on a few exotic holidays and cleared out the local jewellers, the novelty is likely to wear off. Your life will lack meaning and, well, you'll get bored. Look at the many young actors and pop stars who have struggled to cope with sudden fame and fortune, and turned to drugs or alcohol as a way to get their kicks. Furthermore, the popular press delights in telling the stories of hapless lottery winners whose lives have fallen apart because of jealous friends and families, overindulgence and the overall stress of suddenly having a massive life change thrust upon them.

Human beings have a primaeval need to strive. Once upon a time it was hunting and gathering; now it's earning money to support ourselves and our families. Take that away that motivation completely and what is the meaning of life? Whether you win the lottery or retire at 65, you run a very real risk of struggling to fill your days and be happy and fulfilled.

So maybe retirement – in the traditional stop work at 65, wear slacks and spend your days playing bowls way – isn't all it's cracked up to be. What's the alternative then? Well, how about if you could enjoy every day of your life, starting now, combining earning a living with doing what you enjoy? Or even better, making a living doing what you enjoy? If you manage to cram four times as much as most people into an 80-year lifespan, then it's like living to 320 – that's the secret of longevity right there. All you need to do is join the growing number of people who have decided to become lifesavers.

Ask people what their ideal life would be, and most would say something along the lines of "Being able to do what I want when I want." Some talk about a 'work/life balance' but I don't like that term. If 'work' isn't part of your 'life', then what the heck is it? Death maybe? The term 'work/leisure balance' makes more sense and this book shows you how to achieve this. It does, though, go even further and blur the boundaries between 'work' (earning money in other words) and 'leisure' (having a good time) which will allow you to enjoy almost every moment of your life. The ultimate aim is to blur the boundaries so much that work and leisure combine into one happy entity. Remember the old hippy ideals of rebelling and living an alternative lifestyle? Well, this book is all about doing just that, being a 21st-century hippy but without the loons and sandals (unless you really feel the need...). Drop out without dropping out!

You may be reading this thinking that it's too late for you because you're too old and have already spent too many years in a job you dislike. It's better to start off your adult life enjoying it to the full, but it's never too late. In fact the, older you are, the more important it is to make the most of the years you have left. Whether you're 20, 50, or even beyond the traditional age of retirement, there are ideas in this book that you can embrace today to enhance your life. Don't feel that you need to use all the ideas I suggest; some just may not appeal to you or work for you. No matter; if you just go away inspired by one chapter or even by one suggestion from these pages, then my job is done. And, unlike some self-help books, I've kept this one refreshingly short and to the point, so you don't have to spend too much time reading it. And remember; if you want it enough, you can make freedom work for you.

So turn the page and become a lifesaver today.

Chapter One
Why do we work when we do?

"I want to be young and wild, and then I want to be middle-aged and rich, and then I want to be old and annoy people by pretending that I'm deaf."
Edmond Blackadder

Before we start to save our life, it's useful for lifesavers to understand how the current system evolved of working eight hours a day for 40-odd years followed by retirement. And, more importantly, why it's no longer relevant.

The idea of a retirement age came, rather surprisingly, from an extreme right-wing government. It was introduced in Germany in 1889 when Chancellor Otto von Bismarck – a dashing figure who, today, is more famous for creating the German Empire – was trying to fend off the Marxists and wanted to appease his troublesome working classes. The outspoken statesman's radical solution was to set an age of 65 as the time for people to stop work and to start receiving a state pension; a novelty no country had offered before. However, he wasn't doing it simply to be nice to his public but rather as a way to keep the working classes happy and to stop them from voting for the competing socialist party. Why 65? For the simple reason, Bismarck knew that few workers would live much beyond that age so his government wouldn't have to fork out too much in social security payments. Brilliant, if morally suspect.

The thinking behind Bismarck's idea may have been far from kind and caring but, nonetheless, Germany was way ahead of the rest of the planet with its retirement planning. Over the years, though, most of the developed world followed suit and set a retirement age which, in most cases, was close to Germany's 65. In the UK, the Old-Age Pensions Act 1908 provided a pension for everyone over the age of 70 which, back then, must have been a very safe bet indeed for the treasury coffers.

But what happened before Germany's right-wing government came up with a surprisingly socialist idea? Well, long ago, generally people didn't live long enough even to think about stopping work. You were born, went off hunting and gathering until you picked up some nasty disease, were eaten by a nasty animal, or met with a nasty accident. Even if you avoided any such nasties, you'd be lucky to make it beyond your mid-twenties in prehistoric times.

As years went on, life expectancy increased. In Medieval Britain, if you could make it through the maze of deadly childhood illnesses (sadly, 70 percent of kids died before reaching adulthood), there'd be a reasonable chance of you making it to the grand old age of 60. But – and it was a big but – only if you were an aristocrat who didn't need to toil in the fields (or, indeed, in your own home). Because you had a life of leisure, retirement wasn't an issue because you'd never worked in the first place (unless you were called upon by the king or queen to go off to fight in some pesky war, in which case your life expectancy would take a bit of a hit).

Even at the start of the 20th century, when the idea of retirement was taking hold around Europe and North America, the average person was unlikely to live much beyond 65. Which was good news for government funds in countries that were handing out pensions, especially as it was the poor who tended to die first. However, by the end of the same century, improvements in healthcare and living standards meant that you'd be unlucky not to live beyond 65 – way beyond. Today in the UK, the average life expectancy is 81 and rising, yet the age of retirement has only increased by two years to 67, even though many people today are as fit and spritely at that age as they were at 50.

Which is surprising considering that the majority of those people would have spent most of their lives working at least eight hours a day, five days a week. The idea of a 'nine to five' job or 'eight-hour day' is so ingrained in our culture that it's rarely questioned, yet, just like the age of retirement, it has its roots in a very different world to that which we live in today.

Back in the days when most working people toiled on the land, they would rise with the lark and work until either they'd done what they had to do, or the light was failing. There wasn't a distinction between work and leisure – you just did what had to be done, and historical evidence suggests that, in fact, rural workers had considerable more downtime than we do today. In fact, go back even further in time, and it seems that our hunter-gatherer ancestors spent less than five hours a day in the foraging and hunting game. I guess they spent the rest of the day happily picking fleas off each other.

This all changed with the Industrial Revolution, which began in the UK in the mid-18th century, and transformed the way that society in the UK – and, in time, the rest of the western world and beyond – worked. Huge new factories and mines sprang up and, despite some automation, these required scores of people to toil in them. The factory owners were often greedy and wanted to get their full pound of flesh from their minions, who were expected to work for as much as 16 hours a day in grim conditions and for little financial reward.

The wealthy landed gentry, on the other hand, had their own problem – boredom. The ladies and gentlemen struggled to fill their days in their big stately homes, as society insisted that they conducted themselves in a certain way, and there was only so much one could do with some embroidery and a harpsichord. Still, I'm sure the brow-beaten lower classes didn't feel too sorry for them.

It was a Welshman, socialist Robert Owen, who campaigned for limited hours for factory workers. Owen was one of those people who managed to cram a lot into his life – a true lifesaver if ever there was one. He started off working in a drapers' shop, then he got into the spinning business and was elected to the Manchester Board of Health which aimed to help workers' conditions. Owen later moved to Scotland where he was part-owner of a mill that offered its workers generous rights, including childcare for infants – a world first. Then he headed to America where he formed a utopian community before settling in London to lead a socialist association. Finally, in his eighties, Owen became a spiritualist and chatted to the spirits of, among others, Benjamin Franklin and Thomas Jefferson about his plans for world peace! It was while he was in Manchester that Owen began demanding a ten-hour day for factory workers, but he later had some poetic inspiration and dropped that to eight hours, with the snappy slogan "Eight hours labour, Eight hours recreation, Eight hours rest". If maths isn't your strong point, that adds up neatly to 24 hours. So the reason we work eight hours a day is all because of a Welsh soundbite.

Initially, though, Owen's radical ideas were only adopted in the case of children. The Factory Act of 1833 stated that youngsters from the ages of nine to 13 could only work eight hours a day, and those aged 14 to 18 had to clock out after 12 hours toil. This seems horrendous to us today but, back then, it was a vast improvement on the unrestricted situation that came before it. By 1847, women and children were limited to 10 hours work a day, while the hard-done-by men still had to work as long as their bosses demanded. Today, the UK has a 48-hour limit to the working week, but that is not mandatory – employees can choose to work longer hours if they want to but, crucially, their bosses can't force them to do so.

What also happened during the Industrial Revolution was that the holiday was invented. People were given the chance to have a break from work and head off to the coast on one of the new-fangled railways for a refreshing dip in the sea, a stroll along the promenade and the chance to buy a saucy postcard or two. Previously, the idea of stopping work for a week or so was unheard of. You worked six days a week – Sundays had been a day of rest in the UK and other Christian countries since the Middle Ages – all year round. In 1871, though, the UK's Bank Holidays Act gave workers a heady four days off a year. Then, over time, unions negotiated further holidays for its members and this gradually led to the typical 28 days of paid holiday which UK workers enjoy today. However, it wasn't until as late as 1996 that employees in the UK gained a statutory right to 28 days off. Even today, in the USA there is no such statutory holiday entitlement; days off are often dependent on length of service, and the average is just nine days' leave a year.

Weekends were unheard of until surprisingly recently. The Oxford English Dictionary says that the word 'weekend' first appeared in 1879 and, to start with, workers in the UK took Monday off in addition to the traditional Sunday day of rest. This was called Saint Monday but, in reality, was often somewhat less than saintly, with people spending their wages (which they'd collected on the Saturday) on copious amounts of alcohol. Pubs weren't open on Sunday, so this was workers' one day to let their hair down and enjoy their hard-earned cash. In the USA, the Jewish community observed Saturday as the Sabbath day and so unions campaigned successfully for factory workers to take both Saturday and Sunday off so that Jews and Christians would all be able to practice their faith. Henry Ford was one of the first employers to embrace this idea, although he had an ulterior motive; as well as wanting to treat his workers well, he could see that he could sell more cars if people had more time to enjoy them and head off on weekend road trips. One hundred years later, most of the western world still uses this same model of five days working and two days off. Some companies give staff Friday afternoons off but usually only by increasing the time they work Mondays to Thursdays to make up the hours.

Since the 1970s, some UK organisations have offered staff flexitime which lets them choose when they work. However, there is usually a core period when staff have to be at their workplace, allowing them to, say, come in late and go home late to ensure that they accrue the required number of hours per week. This enables employees to, for instance, avoid travelling in the rush-hour and helps them to fit their working hours around their family life.

Another relatively new concept is commuting. Before the industrial revolution, most people lived within walking distance of the farm or wherever they worked. Then, when factories came along, thousands of terraced houses were built close by, so clog-sparking workers could plod their way to and from their dark satanic mills. When the railways arrived, though, wealthier employees, such as managers, would choose to live in the leafy new suburbs, away from the smell and noise of the factories (and, indeed, the common people) and travel into work every morning, feeling smug and superior as they read The Times cocooned in a wood-lined railway carriage. This, then, was the beginning of the middle classes and, today, it's become almost the norm for people to commute 30 miles or more to work and back, usually by train or car.

We are in the high-tech 21st century when we have excellent communication around the world and lots of labour-saving devices, but we still base our working lives on ideas from the world of over 100 years ago. In the 1950s, futurists predicted that by the 21st-century people would only have to work about four hours a day because machines would do much of the toil. Yet here we are in the future with, until recently, undreamt of technology – washing machines, dishwashers, even robot vacuum cleaners, not to mention computers and smartphones – but most of us are working longer hours than ever, rather than enjoying ourselves. That, when you think about it, is a crazy situation but, the good news is, there is plenty lifesavers can do to change it to their advantage; by as little or as much as they like. Read on to find out how.

Quickly...
• The age of retirement was set by a German fascist.
• The eight-hour week was dreamt up by a Welsh socialist.

- Holidays and weekends arrived in the 19th century.
- All of the above are becoming increasing irrelevant in today's hi-tech connected world.
- You can choose to embrace modern technology to work fewer hours.

Chapter Two
Small changes to make the best use of your time

"One day, you're 17 and you're planning for someday. And then quietly, without you ever really noticing, someday is today. And then someday is yesterday. And this is your life."
John Green

Later on in the book, I'll look at some radical changes you can make to ensure that you embrace life to the full. For now, though, let's gently ease you into making better use of the time you have. Here are some easy ways that you can free up some hours every week, so you'll be able to begin to enjoy right now some of those things you've been dreaming of doing when you retire.

A lot of brilliant physicists and philosophers have written learned papers trying to explain what time is and whether or not it actually exists. Which is all very well but what I know is that when I look at my watch, I can see that I have 24 hours in my day, out of which I like to spend eight hours asleep, so that leaves 16 hours for me to do what I have to do and what I want to do. And do you know what? You, me and every other person on this planet has exactly the same 24 hours every day to work with. Our poetic friend from the last chapter, Robert Owen, campaigned for "Eight hours labour, Eight hours recreation, Eight hours rest", which was all very noble but in today's world (and probably in Robert's, too) there are other things that have to be done each day. You may have kids to get to school, meals to cook, clothes to wash, a vacuum cleaner to push around, a car to take in for a service and, not least, a commute to work. All of which has to be taken out of that eight hours which Mr Owen allocated to leisure, plus something our Welsh Victorian didn't have – a weekend.

So, assuming that, for now, you're stuck with an eight-hour, nine to five job, and you enjoy a good night's kip, then you're not left with much time for leisure activities – in other words doing what you want to do, as you would when retired. The trick that lifesavers do is to make the best use of that eight-hour slot by not wasting what non-work time they have.

You may think that you don't waste time, but are you sure? Try this little exercise for a week; each day, keep a notebook with you and, from the moment you wake up until you go to bed keep a note of what you do during every half hour interval. Don't hold back either – note down how long you spend on the toilet, in the shower, eating breakfast, reading the paper, browsing Facebook, travelling to work, watching television and, well, you get the picture. Also, note down whenever you're not really doing anything – daydreaming, waiting for a train, lying on the sofa – you may be surprised at the results.

"I logged my activities over a typical day and was astonished to find that I spent two and a half hours doing pretty much nothing," admits Tom. "Even when I was at the office, I found that I wasted time paper shuffling, chatting to colleagues, staring into space and browsing Facebook. In the evening, I did pretty much nothing worthwhile between getting home and going out for dinner with friends. I watched some rubbish on TV, fiddled with my phone and spent far too long in the shower."

I'm not suggesting you don't do nothing occasionally, as downtime is important, but it's all too easy, without realising it, to spend half an hour browsing Facebook or YouTube when, actually, you could have used that same 30 minutes to do something you really wanted to do; or something you had to do, thus freeing up time for later. And once you become aware of the time you're wasting, you are in a strong position to live smarter, in both your work and your leisure times. What's more, these little snatches of lost time add up to a surprising number of hours, as our friend Tom discovered.

Just imagine what you could do with an extra two and half hours in a day: Fit in an extra two and half hours of work; read a good book; play some golf; cut the lawn; go for a meal, visit a museum; work out at the gym; go on a bike ride. The list is limited only by your imagination. In fact, with the exception of the first suggestion, these are all things that people often say they'd like to spend more time doing 'when they retire'. Why wait when lifesavers do it now?

But, you might point out, you're still stuck with fixed hours at work in your nine to five job. Fair comment and it's something I'll come back to later in the book. For now, though, why not make good use of your eight hours a day at work to, well, work? Increasingly, people find that they have too much to do within their supposed working day, so end up taking tasks home with them, which eats into their evenings. That could be avoided by working more efficiently in the office. And even if that's not the case with you, being efficient in your workplace will make your job less stressful as you will feel more in control and on top of everything that needs doing. Hey, it might even lead to a promotion. Even if you don't enjoy your job, you'll find that you will cope with it better if you put your heart into it and make an effort, rather than lazing around and wasting time. Use the tips in this book to help you to make better use of your working days.

Robert is a lecturer at a further education college and forever found himself bringing work home, much to the annoyance of his family. "I had lectures to plan and essays to mark," he explains. "I'd often be working at home well into the night just to keep on top of everything. I got cross with my kids for bothering me when all they wanted was to spend time with their dad, while my poor wife just felt neglected."

Robert decided something had to change. "I love my job, but I didn't like bringing work home, so I decided to make some changes. I looked at my days and realised that I was wasting time at work. When I didn't have lectures, I'd be in the staffroom, drinking coffee and chatting with colleagues, which was very nice but not particularly productive. Socialising at work is important, so I still do it but do my best to limit it to 20 minutes in the morning when we all arrive at college, plus 20 minutes during our lunch break before making my excuses and finding an empty room I can hide in and get stuck in with some work. I stay on for an hour at the end of most days, too. These simple changes have freed up two and a half hours on a typical day which I can spend doing the work I was previously taking home. Sure, I still occasionally have to do some work at home, but that's now the exception rather than the norm. Our family life has improved immeasurably, and I finally feel like a proper father and husband."

Knuckling down to work isn't just about avoiding distractions, you should also concentrate on one task at a time, rather than jumping from one thing to another. It's been proven that switching from one project to another can waste 20 percent of your day, so it's far better to crack on with one thing and get it finished. Not only is that more efficient, but it's also a great feeling to be able to draw a line under a task – think of it as working one inch wide and one mile deep. And be ruthless about this; if you have a big project to complete, then schedule in, say, four hours of each day to devote to it and work single-mindedly on getting that done, avoiding as many distractions as you possibly can. Turn to Chapter Six for help on doing this.

It's not just your working hours you need to monitor, either. What about your evenings and weekends? Most people watch television to relax which is great but do try to be selective in your viewing. Today's technology allows you to record programmes and films, or download them to watch on demand, either on a television or even on your tablet or smartphone. There's no excuse, then, for just having the television on for the sake of it – you could be watching something you really want to see. What's more, if you always watch recorded programmes you can fast forward through the adverts to save time.

Make good use of what time you have, and you'll have more time to live your life to the full. It makes so much sense, but it's amazing how many people waste, not only, their days but their lives also. And yet, with a bit of planning and tweaking, you can reduce the number of mundane tasks you have to do and set yourself free to embrace life to the full.

Once again, technology is the lifesaver's friend here, enabling you to multitask in ways you'd never have thought possible a few years ago. Most of us spend time travelling, usually by car or train, and this is an ideal time for learning or reading. How so? By listening to audiobooks and podcasts. There is a wealth of self-help and educational books available to download. So if you want to improve your life, pick up a new language or even learn to fly, there's an audiobook for you. Alternatively, why not use your travel time to listen to all those novels you never seem to find a chance to sit down to read? It makes a pleasant change from inane local radio presenters.

It's not just when you're travelling you can listen to audiobooks. How about plugging your earbuds in while you're at the gym – yes, you can get fit and learn how to improve your memory at the same time – or practice your German verbs while cooking dinner? You could even listen to audiobooks via earphones while pushing a trolley around the supermarket.

Actually, here's an even better idea; rather than go to the supermarket for your groceries, order them online and have them delivered to your home. Most major UK supermarkets offer this service and, once you've set up an account with your favourite items, it's 15 minutes' work once a week to order your groceries and they'll then be delivered to your door. How does that compare with driving to the supermarket, parking the car, going from aisle to aisle hunting down that elusive tin of beans, queuing up to pay, then loading it all into the car and driving home again? It's just a shame the delivery driver won't put the food in your kitchen cupboards and fridge for you as well... Oh, and to ensure that you do actually order a full week's shop and don't end up having to make trips to the supermarket to pick up those little things you forget to have delivered, get into the habit of keeping a shopping list to hand (ideally on your smartphone) and whenever you think of something you need, add it to the list immediately.

Online shopping goes much further than groceries, too. Being a bloke, I'd be quite happy never to set foot in a shop again and, for the last few years, have successfully done all my Christmas shopping online, thus avoiding the usual festive scrum. And it's not just at Christmas; buying via the Internet not only frees up valuable time to do the things you really want to do, but it also has the added happy benefit of being environmentally friendly, as it drastically cuts down on car journeys. Look around a typical supermarket car park at the sheer number of cars that are there, most of which could – and should – be replaced by a small fleet of delivery trucks taking efficient routes around the district.

Sadly, the Internet can't help with all household chores but you can farm work out. Cleaners and gardeners aren't only for the wealthy – if you find yourself scrubbing the toilet on a weekend when you should be out having fun, maybe it's time to consider employing a cleaner. Look it as offsetting some of the hours you spend earning money so, in effect, you're reducing your working hours. Confused? Trust me, it makes sense. Say, for argument's sake, you earn £30 an hour yourself, and a cleaner costs £10 an hour, you have to work an extra 20 minutes to cover the cost of an hour's toilet cleaning. Alternatively, you take an effective £10 drop in income to cover the cost of not having to attack skid marks at the weekend. The same logic can be applied to gardening (assuming, that is, that's not something you enjoy – I guess no one yearns to clean toilets), car washing, window cleaning and, indeed, any chore.

If you can afford it, paying someone else to do what you don't want to do, not only makes sense, it helps others, too. Indeed, there's a good chance that the people you will use have, themselves, improved their lives by taking control and becoming self-employed. If fact, if you enjoy, say, mowing lawns or cleaning cars, this could work to your benefit – see Chapter Ten.

Alternatively, if you have children, rope them into working around the house and garden. You could pay them, or you could simply insist that they do their bit to help run the family home. Either way, it will instil a work ethic in them, encourage them to respect their home and, crucially, free up quality time for you all which, in turn, will improve your relationship with your family.

Outsourcing can also help with your professional life. If you work for yourself, it's easy to get bogged down with mundane admin tasks, such as bookkeeping which, for not much money, you can get someone else to do. That then frees you up to either do some productive work or, even better, spend time on your favourite leisure activity.

If you're reading this thinking, "I'll give some of these ideas a go sometime," then you've fallen into the classic trap of procrastination – putting off doing something. This is a surefire way to waste time and can also lead to stress as essential tasks pile up and you end up panicking when something becomes urgent. In an ideal world, you should have nothing critical to do because you would have completed all your important jobs before they became pressing. Turn to Chapter Six to find out how to deal with procrastination – now!

It's inevitable that you'll have to deal with some unexpected urgent tasks from time to time, but if you ensure that you are always up to date with other jobs, then you'll be able to accommodate the unexpected when it comes up. That said, it's good to learn to say 'no' from time to time. It's very easy – especially if you work for yourself – to never turn jobs down but you have to be realistic. If you don't have the time – or indeed the inclination – to do something you've been asked to do, politely decline it, delegate it, or schedule it into your diary for another day.

Quickly...
- We all have the same 24 hours a day to work with.
- Monitor your time over two weeks and analyse where you're wasting it.
- Stop wasting time and use what you save to do something you enjoy.
- Make good use of your working hours and you'll become more efficient.
- Listen to audiobooks and podcasts while you're doing other things.
- Shop online rather than wasting time at supermarkets and shops.

- Outsource tasks you don't want to do, freeing up time for yourself.
- Learn to turn down work.

Chapter Three
Plan your time

"You only live once, but if you do it right, once is enough"
Mae West

How do lifesavers avoid wasting time? By planning their time, that's how. And the way to do that is to use a diary and a to-do list. As you'll read in Chapter Five, I like to use electronic calendars and to-do lists, as they work with me to save even more time. However, if you prefer a paper diary, that's fine – just ensure that you can carry one with you all the time, and it has room in it for your to-do lists. Businesses use diaries and planners to be organised and efficient, and you as an individual should be no different.

There's a fair chance you already use a diary of some description but do you use it to the full? Have a look in it now. Worst case scenario is that it's empty or just has details of birthdays and bank holidays. Ah, you say, not true – you have all your work appointments in your diary and refer to it religiously. If so, that's great and you're well on your way to being organised. However, you can take your diary use to a whole higher level in the quest to be time-efficient.

As well as work appointments, I'm rather hoping that you also have your social life in your diary – that dinner party with Steve and Beckie next Saturday night, for instance. If not, you should do, otherwise you have to remember all this stuff in your head, which inevitably leads to awkward double bookings, and creates stress as you try to recall everything that's happening in your life.

So if your diary isn't already populated with all your work and social appointments, get them in there now. And don't forget to liaise with colleagues and family to ensure there are no clashes (another advantage of electronic diaries is that you can share them).

How's the diary looking now? You may have that meeting with the boss from 10am to 11am on Tuesday, which you're dreading almost as much as that dental appointment at 3pm on Wednesday, but at least you're out at the cinema with friends on Friday and, oh look, don't forget it's Auntie Flo's birthday at the weekend, so you'd better get a card in the post.

Already your life's looking more organised but look again at your calendar. I bet you've still got plenty of empty spaces in there. What are you doing during that time? "Ah, there's nothing planned for then," you say. So what are you going to do? "Well, the usual stuff, work, relax, maybe go to the gym if I've time, and I'd really like to squeeze in a round of golf." Sound familiar? "If I've time" is a statement we frequently use in conjunction with something that we'd really like to do and, invariably, we end up not having the time for. Or rather, we don't make the time for because we've been busy doing, well, not very much or allowed another task to take over.

What's the solution then? Well, get those things in the diary. If you want to hit the gym three evenings a week, block off one hour for three nights on your calendar (an electronic diary will allow you set repeating events, so every week these three evenings are automatically booked for you). The same for that round of golf or whatever else you'd like to do.

You can also plan your work time like this. Do you have a report to write but keep putting it off or getting distracted by other things? Then block off a couple of hours to dedicate to getting it done. I got this book written by using my electronic diary to allocate a couple of hours a day to it and ensuring that I did this and nothing else during that time each and every day.

The key to ensuring that diary keeping will be a success is to stick to your bookings. When a mate rings up to see if you're free for a pint on Wednesday night, check your diary first and, if you're booked to go to the gym, then you're not free to socialise until later that evening, or maybe arrange to see your friend another day when you do have time (just make sure you note it in the diary!). The key is to treat everything – and I mean everything – in your diary as sacrosanct.

Paul started to make full use of the calendar on his smartphone a year ago and confesses to being addicted to it now. "I used to be hopeless at managing my time," he admits. "I'm a magazine editor and, despite knowing that I have a deadline every month, I'd always be working late at the last minute each month to get the next issue out, with all-nighters not being uncommon. I really was going to the wire!"

However, once Paul started to use his calendar to organise his workflow, things improved immeasurably. "I realised that I had X number of pages to produce each month and X number of days to do them," Paul explains. "So I simply did the maths and worked out how many pages I needed to create each day, and blocked off time in the diary to do them. This diary is shared with everyone on the team, and we use shared spreadsheets to monitor the workflow, so we can see if we're falling behind and, if so, we can do something about it."

Paul's adopted the old adage "How do you eat an elephant – one bite at a time" and it's not only changed his work but his whole life. "I'm so much more relaxed at work now," he says. "There are no last-minute rushes, so I rarely have to work late – and certainly not overnight – and this has improved my home life, too, as I see more of my wife and kids and am less stressed around them, too."

In fact, Paul now has his whole family converted to electronic calendars. "We each have an Android phone with shared Google Calendars, so we all know what's going on. I know when my son needs a lift to football and my daughter knows she can't go to her boyfriend's on evenings when we need her to babysit our youngest. We all put everything in our diaries because we know if we don't, it can mess things up for the whole family." You can discover more about how electronic diaries can help you save your life in the next chapter.

Another advantage of using a diary to schedule your time is that it forces you to get things done in the time allocated. Back in the 1950s, an English author and historian called Cyril Northcote Parkinson came up with a rule which he modestly called Parkinson's Law. The law states that "Work expands so as to fill the time available for its completion" and was initially an observation on the inefficiencies of the public sector but he went on, in a best-selling book of the same name, to suggest that it's a malady that affects most of us. If we're given an eight-hour day and a certain amount of work to do, we'll subconsciously ensure that it will take us the full eight hours to do that job. On the other hand, if we were limited to just six hours we'd miraculously manage to do the same amount in the shorter time.

Nicola discovered this in her job as a human resources manager: "Like most people, I work an eight-hour day, five days a week," she explains. "However, it's all too easy to stay late in the office which is just what I got into the habit of doing, often working until seven o'clock or later. Then, after my first child was born, I decided to be more disciplined and leave promptly at five thirty every evening. Amazingly, I found that I was doing the same amount of work during the shorter days."

Parkinson's Law is even more likely to kick in if you're self-employed, as car mechanic Richard explains: "I found myself working seven days a week at my garage, for the simple reason I could. Then I found myself a girlfriend and she insisted that I took weekends off, so I was forced to be more efficient during the week and I'm pleased to say that my income hasn't suffered at all, and I'm enjoying my free time at the weekends."

It really is essential to put limits on your working hours and, by doing so, you will free up time to spend doing what you enjoy. Gail is a freelance writer and used to feel guilty if she wasn't in the office: "I'd start work at nine every morning and plod through to five o'clock just because I felt that's what I was meant to do," she confesses. "However, I only earn what amounts to a part-time income, so I made the decision to work just three days a week, because that then equates to a reasonable hourly wage." Gail is strict about her new working hours and does a nine to five day in the office on Mondays, Tuesdays and Wednesdays, then has a four day weekend. What a great balance and, crucially, Parkinson's Law did its thing and she's now doing the same amount of work and bringing in the same income. "I'm simply more focused because I know I only have three days a week in which to earn a living," says Gail. "Before, I'd be faffing around checking Facebook and spending too much time on the phone to clients, but now I knuckle down and do the job I have to do."

Reducing your working day from five to three days is impressive but how about squeezing it even further? According to the Pareto Principle, 80 percent of your results comes from 20 percent of your effort? What, you may ask, is the Pareto Principle? Well, it's all down to some garden peas. At the end of the 19th century, an Italian economist and philosopher by the name of Vilfredo Pareto noticed, as you would, that 20 of the pea pods in his garden created 80 percent of his crop of peas and went on to note that 80 percent of Italy's land was owned by 20 percent of the population, which didn't sit well with his socialist principles. Other people later applied this same 80/20 principle to other areas, including business, and discovered it fitted perfectly. In fact, it seems that most of life follows the Pareto Principle.

For instance, Richard Koch in his book, *Living Life the 80/20 Way*, points out that 80 percent of problems can be attributed to 20 percent of causes; 80 percent of a company's profits come from 20 percent of its customers; 80 percent of a company's complaints come from 20 percent of its customers; 80 percent of a company's profits come from 20 percent of its staff's time; 80 percent of a company's sales come from 20 percent of its products; 80 percent of a company's sales are made by 20 percent of its sales staff.

How does this help with your time management? Look at what you spend your time doing and you will discover that you also live by the Pareto Principle. You may find that, say, 80 percent of your income is generated during 20 percent of your working time, and the remainder of your day is spent on non-productive tasks. Or 20 percent of what you do gives you 80 percent of your enjoyment. How about, then, you could change this so that 80 percent of your income was generated over 20 percent of your entire waking day, leaving the other 80 percent of the day to do what you want in?

As we discovered in Chapter One, the only reason we work eight hours a day is because of a poetic Welshman. So many office workers spend the last hour or so of their working day twiddling their thumbs and waiting for the clock to hit 5.30pm so they can grab their coats and get the hell out of the office, simply because they don't think it's worth starting on anything else. Conversely, if they are really busy and in the middle of something, they'll stop what they are doing at bang-on 5.30pm and leave. It's a crazy situation and inefficient. If you've done what you need to do, then go home. If you have a lot to do, then work a bit later, rather than being a clock watcher. Sadly, some companies insist that staff work set hours, but even then, you can be efficient and actually work until your finish time, which will mean you can hit the ground running when you go in the next morning.

Which then begs the question, why work from 9 to 5 if you don't have to? Why not fit work in around the rest of your life, rather than following a timetable that has its origin in Victorian times? Steve is a freelance feature writer for technology magazines and works when it suits him: "On weekdays I'm up at 7am as my kids leave for school at 7.45," he explains. "I used to faff around until 9am before starting work. Then I realised that I was wasting an hour. I now use that time to good effect, catching up on emails and doing some writing, before I get interrupted by phone calls, and I get a surprising amount done in that short time. So much so, in fact, I'm often tempted to stop work at 10am and, if the weather is good, I'll head off for a spot of jet-skiing. Luckily, I have a couple of friends nearby who also work for themselves, so I can usually persuade one of them to join me for some high-speed fun. What's the point of being stuck in an office when the weather is good?" That's a good point that Steve makes and he's an excellent example of living life to the full. He admits he does work hard, though: "Some people think I'm shirking when I'm off having a laugh, but actually I do have to knuckle down to earn a living – jet skis don't come cheap! While other people are crashed out on the sofa watching Eastenders in the evening, you'll find me slaving in front of my Mac writing about computers and gadgets for magazines and websites. The difference is, I make good use of my daylight hours."

When you're working on a task, especially an onerous one, promise to treat yourself when it's finished. It doesn't have to be anything glamorous, expensive high-brow – maybe 20 minutes browsing Facebook, watching your favourite TV programme or even eating a particularly naughty doughnut. It's good to dangle a carrot (or sugary treat) in front of you to encourage you to get things done. If it's a bigger project over a period of weeks, then give yourself a larger reward – maybe a meal out with a loved one, a weekend away, a new outfit, or a day trip out on the motorbike. The human mind responds well to working towards a reward.

Quickly...

• Get a diary and use it for all your work and social appointments.

• Put in your diary stuff that you want to do each week and stick to it.

• Limit the amount of time you spend on a project and you'll do it without that time.

• Choose to work when it suits you, rather than from 9 to 5.

Save Your Life www.saveyourlife.me

-

Chapter Four
Making lists

"Life is inherently risky. There is only one big risk you should avoid at all costs, and that is the risk of doing nothing"
Denis Waitley

We all have things to do every day, whether we're working, retired or unemployed. And there's a fair chance that you make a to-do list to help you through the day, even if it's just in your mind. However, there's also a fair chance that you're not making the best use of this list. Lists are great and an essential part of having an organised life (in other words, one that makes the best use of your time so you can achieve more). The lifesaver's trick is not to just have one to-do list, but rather a number of lists to cover various aspects of your life.

Let's start with work. All jobs are different, and there are obviously some where a to-do list perhaps isn't needed. If you're on a checkout in a supermarket, for instance, you know that you have to scan the goods, chat to the customers, and process the payments; there's no need to list any of that. At the other extreme, if you're an airline pilot, you have checklists that you have to adhere to at various times throughout your working day to ensure that everything works as planned and you and your passengers are safe.

Let's assume that your job is somewhere in the middle, and this could apply whether you're, say, a manager in an office, a farmer in a field, or a school teacher in a classroom. You will have various tasks you have to do that day, and making a list of what needs to be done is a great way of focussing the mind and helping you to get on with your day. Sure, various other unscheduled things are bound to crop up but keep concentrating on that list and don't stop until you've ticked everything off.

But, I hear you say, you have a to-do list and never manage to tick off all the items – it's never-ending! That's because your list needs managing. Here's how to do it.

First of all, write down everything you have to do in your life – and I mean everything, from writing that sales report for the boss to fixing the dripping tap in the bathroom. As you do this, split the items into general groups, such as work, home, hobbies and family. It's going to appear overwhelming at this point, but it really isn't – you need to dump everything out of your brain and onto paper – yes, as much as I like technology, at this early stage good old-fashioned paper is best, but you'll soon be loading up your electronic to-do list (see Chapter Five) if that's how you prefer to work.

Now look through the list and consider each item. A to-do item should, ideally, be a task that you can complete in no more than an hour or two – some may only take a few minutes, but others could be longer. You'll probably have some items on your list which need to be broken down into smaller chunks. For instance, "Paint the bathroom" could, if you wish, be divided into a number of to-do items – "Choose a colour", "Buy paint and brushes", "Paint bathroom", although you may be happy enough just to leave it as "Paint the bathroom", as it's fairly obvious that you need to choose a colour and buy some paint. On the other hand, once a job gets any more complicated than that, you really do need to break it down into its component tasks, otherwise, you'll keep looking at it on your to-do list and it'll become that elephant in the room that you're afraid to think about, never mind eat.

This book is an example of a large project that I had to split into chunks. Adding "Write book" to my to-do list would have been pointless as it's not a task I could do in an hour or two and then tick off as completed, so it would just have sat ignored on my list. Instead, I created a new category on my to-do list called "Write book" and within that I had a list of tasks, including "Write introduction", "Research the history of pensions" and punctuation" Write a chapter on to-do lists". Even some of those were too much, though, so on my must-do for the day list I'd have something like "Write 1000 words on to-do lists". For me, 1000 words is a bite-sized chunk that I can easily manage within the time allocated.

By the way, some people take this division of projects into bite-sized tasks very seriously and follow a system called Getting Things Done (or GTD) after the book of the same name by David Allen. Software and apps have been developed that allow you to manage your tasks using the GTD philosophy, which involves breaking projects down into micro-sized tasks and grouping similar tasks from different projects together. I've tried GTD and it's a little too structured for my life but by all means give it a go yourself – it certainly works for a lot of people.

The next step is to prioritise tasks. You may want to get the bathroom painted by the end of the month when the in-laws visit, for instance, so put a completion date next to that job. Some tasks may not have a deadline at all but you should nonetheless give each one a date by which it has to be done, otherwise there's a fair chance you'll never do it. I remember from my days in magazine publishing that nothing focuses the mind better than a deadline.

So you should now have a number of to-do lists, in various categories, some of which will be projects in their own right. You can then, if you wish, transfer these to an electronic to-do list (see Chapter Five), making sure that you add a due date for each one.

Then, make a must-do list of what you, – yes, you guessed it – must do today, pulling items from your more general to-do lists. If you are using an electronic to-do list on your computer and/or smartphone, any items with that day set as the due date will automatically appear in the list for that particular day and other items will remain hidden. You can start your working day by making your must-do list but it's even better to do it the day before, once you have completed all the tasks on that day's list. That way, you hit the ground running the following morning. In fact, you may want to make the last item on each day's must-do list "Make tomorrow's must-do list". Do this at the end of every day and you'll hit the ground running each morning. You may also want to do a review of the lists at the end of every week so you can see what you've succeeded with and what's got left, and then make a plan for the following Monday – it's like having a progress meeting with yourself.

Note the word 'must' – this is the critical thing. It's not a 'to-do' list you're creating but rather a 'must-do' list. For that particular day, just have in front of you this must-do list and ensure that you complete each of the tasks on it. Once you've done everything on the must-do list you can, if you wish, finish work for the day and get on with something else that you want to do or, if you are in the mood for more work, you can pick other items from your to-do lists and tick off one or two of those, so you get ahead of yourself.

You should also add some of your day's tasks to your diary. You need to be sensible here; there's no point in blocking off time during the day to making a quick phone call but if you need to spend a large chunk of your day on one task, such as producing a report, writing a feature or painting that bathroom, then block off the time in your diary so that you know you're not going to be available to do other things. This is a powerful way of focussing your mind. If you've allocated the morning to doing one particular task, then if anyone asks you to do something else, you can tell them, no, you're already tied up with something else – you don't have to say what – and you'll have to fit them in another time. This applies to work colleagues, family or friends – be really firm when someone tries to drag you away from something that's in your diary.

Some smartphone and computer apps create combined to-do lists and calendars that automatically put your tasks into your calendar. On the other hand, if you don't like electronics, carry a notebook or diary around with you and add your daily must-do list to that. Please, though, don't whatever you do use scraps of paper or the backs of envelopes for your lists – you'll just lose them.

"I'm a big believer in must-do lists," says Peter who runs a small IT and web design company. "I use the wonderful GTD app, Things, on my iPhone, iPad, Mac and Apple Watch, and at the start of each day I review and set up a Today list. The app automatically carries over any incomplete tasks from the previous day but I take great pride in ensuring that rarely happens – I almost always complete everything on my Today list each day. The key to doing this is to assess how long each task will take and never add on more than I know I can achieve in each day. Unexpected tasks inevitably crop up during each day and, where possible, I put these into my to-do list's Inbox for processing another day but, inevitably, some things just can't wait so I always ensure I factor in some slack time to cope with these. Once I've completed my must-do list, I finish work. Sometimes I get everything done by 2pm, which is great as I can have the afternoon off. Other times, if things don't go quite to plan, I could be working until 8pm but I keep at it until the whole list is clear. It's a great feeling when it's done!"

Peter is right about that. I can't stress how powerful a daily must-do list is. Not only is it more manageable than a worryingly long to-do list, but being able to see the end of the list in sight every day means that you will be so much more motivated to get through the tasks and, once you've ticked off the final item, you'll feel remarkably satisfied that you've had a productive and worthwhile day. That's a great feeling which will inspire you to get the things on the list done and out of the way. If you don't work with a must-do list, then you'll never have the pleasure of clearing your to-do list as that's never going to happen – by its very nature, your main to-do list should constantly be evolving with new items being added to it as others are crossed off.

Indeed, it's essential that you add new items to your to-do-list the moment you know about them. No matter how trivial a task may be, add it to your list immediately. To make this easier, I have a holding category or Inbox within my electronic to-do list where I dump all new items as they come in. Then, At the end of each day review the contents of the Inbox and move tasks into their relevant sections.

Don't take this too far, though, or you'll end up listing even the smallest tasks when, in fact, there are times when it's just simpler – and quicker – to just do the job. For instance, you may suddenly realise you need to book the car in for a service; if you're not busy then just pick up the phone and make the booking there and then (remembering to add the date to your diary afterwards). David Allen calls this the Two Minute Rule. If a task is going to take you less then two minutes, then just do it rather than adding it to a list. This is an incredibly powerful rule to live by and means that lots of small jobs just get done before they start to pile up and become a stress. Making phone calls, replying to emails, even loading the dishwasher immediately after you've had a meal are all things that you can do in a couple of minutes and you'll be surprised how much better you feel without them hanging over you. There is more about the Two Minute Rule in Chapter Six.

To-do (and must-do) lists are perfect for getting all those everyday tasks done and will enable you to be more efficient in both your work and your leisure time. However, list making can be taken further to cover those long-term goals and things you want to achieve in life – your bucket list, if you like, all those things you want to do before you kick the bucket. Let's be honest here – most people can substitute the word 'bucket' for 'retirement' but rather than putting off all those great things until you retire, let's work on doing some of them sooner rather than later. These are things like "Sail around the UK", "Visit the Taj Mahal", "Swim with dolphins, "Learn to paint" and "Read *War and Peace.*" Probably not things you can add to your regular to-do list, so you need to make a new list for these life goals. In fact, let's call it your life goal list.

Once again, have a brainstorming session with yourself and get all the things you've ever wanted to do written down on a piece of paper, however crazy some of them may seem. Now go through the list and mark the items in terms of desirability, feasibility and when you'd like to do them. Be honest with yourself here, too. If you're 47 years old, your chances of winning gold at the Olympics in the 1600 metres is unlikely, but you could certainly train to, say, run a marathon. Similarly, becoming an astronaut is pie in the sky for most of us, so how about learning to fly a light aircraft instead? Even the wildest goals can often be modified to become achievable.

On the other hand, other things you've always wanted to do may, in fact, be relatively straightforward to achieve. Going back to reading *War and Peace*, for instance, that is something you could start immediately – these days you don't even need to go a shop to buy the book, you can download it right now onto your reader, tablet or even smartphone, and begin plodding your way through it.

And that is the lifesaver's key to any goal – make a start. Once you've made your list of life goals, pick two that you want to achieve within the next 12 months. Make sure they're ones that you can practically manage – cycling around the world will be tricky to do if you have a family to look after, so that's one to put on the back-burner until you're an empty nester. The goals should be ones that you can realistically do together in the same year: One may be something that will take a lot of your time, say learning a new skill, while the other could simply be a week's holiday to a destination you've always wanted to go to visit.

Now create a new to-do list category and make a list of all the steps you need to do to achieve those goals. If you want to learn to fly, the first thing to do is find out where your local flying school is, then make contact with them and book an introductory lesson (just to make sure you really do want to do it). If you'd like to have a holiday in Nepal, you could bypass the list and go straight online and book it – Carpe Diem! Later, though, lists will be useful in planning the holiday – where to visit, what to take and so on.

Once you've set your two goals, and made associated to-do lists (with due dates), you also need to book time into your diary to devote to them. This can be easy if your goal involves formal sessions (such as the aforementioned flying lessons) but harder in the case of something you're doing more off your own back, such as teaching yourself to paint or training to run a marathon. In the latter case, it's crucial, therefore, that you block off space in the diary to do the necessary practice. That will give you the discipline to stick to what the diary says and stop you from finding excuses to do other things to do instead. Also, try to put something onto your daily must-do list each day that will help you achieve your life's desires.

Your life goal list is probably another that you'll never complete. You'll add new items to it and, as time goes on, you'll find that your desires will change and some things you'll never achieve. No worries, though, other ambitions will come along to take their place. Just do the things that feel right to you at the time.

Quickly…
- Make a list of everything you have to do.
- Divide the tasks into groups – home, work, etc.
- Break bigger jobs into management chunks.
- Each day make a must-do list and ensure you are able to do all the tasks within that day.
- Block out time in your diary for your daily tasks.
- When a new task comes in, add it to your to-do list immediately.
- If a job is only going to take two minutes or less, do it straight away.
- Make a list of things you really want to achieve in your life.
- Pick two of those things to achieve this year – and then make a start.

Chapter Five
Your own personal assistant

"For the past 33 years, I have looked in the mirror every morning and asked myself: 'If today were the last day of my life, would I want to do what I am about to do today?' And whenever the answer has been 'No' for too many days in a row, I know I need to change something."
Steve Jobs

The rich and famous always seem to have 'people' to assist them. Once upon a time it was valets or ladies in waiting who would help them to dress for dinner, but now, more often than not, the wealthy have personal assistants, or PAs, to organise their diaries, field phone calls and buy presents for their loved ones. Have you ever thought how great it would be to have a personal assistant of your very own? Someone to offload tasks onto, someone who can help to organise your life by telling you what you need to do, where you need to be and remind you of special occasions such as birthdays and anniversaries? Someone who is always at your beck and call to make your days run smoothly 24/7, although maybe not to help you get dressed for dinner…

Well, you may be surprised to know that you probably already have a personal assistant with you right now. In your pocket or in your hand. Yes, if you own a smartphone – and let's face it, most of us do these days – then you have a very powerful device that will help you to organise your life and generally make your days more efficient. And there you were thinking that your phone was just for watching videos of cute kittens.

The smartphone was pre-dated by the PDA (Personal Digital Assistant) which harks back to the Psion Organiser of 1984. This futuristic device was billed as the first pocket computer and could run handy programs including diaries and databases. Over the years, as PDAs became smaller and more powerful, they began to catch on with tech-savvy business types who wanted to remain organised while on the move, although these trendsetters also had to carry a separate (and bulky) mobile phone to be truly up there. The first combined phone and PDA was the short-lived but wonderfully named IBM Simon which appeared in 1994. Then followed the rather more successful Nokia Communicator and the city slicker's favourite, the Blackberry.

However, these early smartphones with their tiny keyboards and clunky operating systems were fiddly and never really caught on with the masses. And then Apple gave us the iPhone, which was a game-changer, not just in terms of mobile phones but also in the way we live our lives. Losing the physical keyboard in favour of a touchscreen that allowed you to interact more naturally with the phone was the key to the iPhone's brilliance, as was the ability to download 'apps' to do various tasks.

Google quickly jumped on the bandwagon with its unashamedly copycat Android operating system and then Microsoft followed suit with its beautiful looking but rather less popular Windows Mobile system. Today, which platform you choose doesn't matter, as they all do much the same thing in terms of helping you to organise your life. Personally, I favour the iPhone for its looks, ease of use and – crucially – the way it interacts with my other devices, namely my MacBook laptop, iPad and Apple Watch. More of which later.

Indeed, a smartphone will enable a lifesaver to work smartly in many more ways than just helping you to be organised. I pretty much run my business via my iPhone, which frees me up to live my life by my terms.

For now, though, let's start with the organisational bit. I've already covered the importance of diaries in

Chapter Three and the ability to have an electronic diary in your pocket all the time is fantastic. What's more, you can share your diary with family and colleagues, so everyone knows what each other is doing. You may not want your fellow workers to know what you get up to on the weekends, so the solution is to set up different diaries for various sections of your life, such as work and family. They'll all appear on your own calendar, but you can decide who, if anyone, sees which one.

However, the key to using an electronic diary is to maximise its full potential. You see, unlike a paper diary, which you have to remember to look at, your smartphone can alert you when an appointment is becoming due, and even work out how long you need to allow to get to where you need to be. All you have to do is make the appointment and add the location, and the phone will do the rest. When you add your alerts, think about when you need reminding – if it's a friend's birthday, for instance, ask for an alert two days before so you can buy a card and present in good time. On the other hand, if you need reminding that the plumber is coming, a 15-minute warning should be enough time for you to put on the kettle. Repeating calendar events, meanwhile, ensure that you'll never miss a birthday or other anniversary ever again.

As I pointed out in Chapter Three, a diary is no good whatsoever unless you add your appointments to it, and here a smartphone makes it so easy. Let's say your partner texts you "I've booked dinner at Wagamama's at 8pm tonight". Your phone will highlight the time and day, and all you need to do is press the link to add it to your diary. Why, it will even add the location and tell you how long you need to get there (and direct you there when the time comes). It's the same with incoming emails, and the calendar will politely point out if a new appointment is going to clash with an existing one. You can also add appointments by typing them in, but most modern smartphones have voice recognition so, just like a human personal assistant, you can speak to them: "Make me an appointment with Joe at one o'clock Wednesday, please," (yes, I know it's only a machine but I like to be polite to it). Smartwatches, such as the Apple Watch, take this one stage further and let you speak to your wrist, so you don't even have to get your phone out of your pocket.

Your smartphone is also the perfect place to keep your to-do list (see Chapter Three) because, once again, it's always with you and will give you reminders when an item is due to be completed. There are countless to-do apps available for smartphones, some of which are remarkably sophisticated and powerful. I've tried a few but I keep coming back to the default Reminders app which is preloaded onto my iPhone. It's simple but effective and powerful, and allows me to have categories for various aspects of my life (cars, writing, home, personal, sailing). Reminders can be set to repeat daily, weekly, monthly or annually, which is very useful for regular tasks (I set one to do my accounts every Friday, otherwise I'd never do them). Even if you have hundreds of items in your to-do list, dividing them into categories like this makes it so much easier to manage them, while a Scheduled view shows just those items which are due today. Once you've completed a task, simply tap it and it will disappear from your list – and there's nothing more satisfying than having an empty to-do list at the end of the day (or, even better, before the end of the day)!

The real genius of calendars and to-do lists on a smartphone is that they can sync with the equivalent lists on your computer and tablet. If you're using Apple devices, this all happens automatically – and near-instantly – via your iCloud account, while other platforms offer similar functionality. This also means that anyone you choose to share your diaries with will also have your latest appointments in front of them as soon as you've made them, and as you move from phone to tablet to laptop, everything is always up to date. It is all very ingenious and makes life so much simpler. Apple's ecosystem also allows you to have reminders and calendars on your wrist if you use an Apple Watch.

It is this power of the internet that allows you to embrace technology to the full to give you real freedom. Take emails for instance; there are few people these days who don't send and receive at least some emails in the course of their work and it's a brilliant way to communicate – much easier than typing a letter, putting it in an envelope and walking down to the postbox. Despite this fantastic convenience, some people complain that having email access on their smartphone, tablet or laptop means that they can never escape from it. Lifesavers, on the other hand, think differently and realise that being able to access their email from anywhere is a huge bonus because it allows you to escape the confines of an office and deal with your emails wherever you are, whenever you want.

The key to efficient email management is to use an IMAP rather than an old-fashioned POP account, as this will ensure that your emails are the same on all your devices (if you're not tech-savvy, ask your internet provider for help changing to this type of account; it really is worth doing). In other words, with an IMAP account, if you delete an email from your smartphone, it will at the same time be removed from your laptop and tablet and this is a massive time saver. Just think about when you check your emails – how many do you read and then delete without having to respond? Indeed, I'll bet there are a fair few dodgy ones you delete without even opening. Being able to do this on your phone in a spare moment – when stuck in a traffic jam or waiting for a train, for instance

– makes good use of time that would otherwise be wasted. When you later get back to your office or home and check your computer, those unwanted emails will be long gone.

Some emails do demand a response and, again, technology allows you to do so wherever you are via your portable device. And here's a handy tip; instead of the usual "Sent from my iPhone" type signature, set one up on your phone and tablet that is identical to the signature on your main computer; that way no one need know that you're sitting on the beach rather than in the office.

This reminds me of a great story – I'm not sure if it's true or not but I certainly hope that it is – about an IT worker at a large company. For a few months, while in his big open-plan office at work, he made sure he was rarely at his desk but somewhere else in the building. Whenever a colleague contacted him by phone or email, he quickly responded, saying he was just around the corner or wherever. He continued to do his job efficiently using his laptop from the canteen, in an empty conference room or at a spare desk. After a few weeks of doing this, he took things one step further and he started working from home, doing exactly the same job, taking calls and answering emails from colleagues, and no one missed his physical presence in the office. Feeling confident, he then headed off to an exotic beach resort and continued to work – as diligently as ever, sitting happily in the sunshine sipping a beer. Again, no one noticed his absence from the office, he did his job efficiently and kept his manager happy without setting foot in his office for months. What a lifesaver!

Today's mobile technology allows you to do much work away from the office more than just managing emails. If you spend time on trains, then you have an excellent opportunity to make good use of the time while you're travelling. This is far from a new concept, of course; get on any commuter train and you'll see plenty of people tapping away on laptops. However, a tablet such as an iPad is even smaller and more convenient to carry around and, once, you get used to typing on a touchscreen it becomes quite natural (if you don't get on with a touchscreen, link a Bluetooth keyboard to your tablet or even to your smartphone). Apps are available to enable to you write, update accounts, or create spreadsheets and presentations, all compatible with the software on your main computer. And cloud computing ensures that all your files are in sync across all your devices. I wrote much of this book using Pages on an iPad (and even some of it on my iPhone) knowing that the latest version would be on my MacBook when I returned to the office. Apple even allows you to move seamlessly from iPad or iPhone to Mac, starting a file or email on one and continuing on another.

All this frees you up to work anywhere – not just on a train. Imagine writing reports while sitting on the beach, in a coffee shop, in the hills, in a tent, or on your yacht. What do you mean you can't afford a yacht? Read Chapter Eight and you may just change your mind.

There's much more you can do with your smartphone or tablet, too. For instance, I use mine for reading books; you can carry a complete library in your pocket and the transmitted light from the screen means that, even if your eyesight isn't perfect, it's possible to read small text much more clearly than on the printed page. I read the news on my phone, too, using a dedicated RSS reader (another great timesaver that pumps feeds from any news sites you're interesting in onto one screen, rather than you having to jump from website to website). I can monitor my website traffic, order goods from Amazon and the local supermarket, check the weather and the tides, and even do my accounts using an app which, again, syncs across all my devices. My smartphone, and its companion watch, really is my own personal assistant that helps me to be super-efficient in both my work and my leisure activities, thus allowing me to make better use of my time.

The lifesaving key to all this is to ensure that your smartphone (and other digital devices) remains a slave to you and not the other way round. So often you see people become slaves to their phones – always staring at the screens when, in fact, they should be engaging with the real world. So, use your smartphone intelligently as your personal assistant but, just like any good employer, make sure you give it some time off every day which, in turn, gives you a break from it. If you find yourself eager to look at your phone from the moment you wake up, then every few minutes throughout the day, then that's a warning sign that you're not having a healthy relationship with it. Take a step back and resist 'checking' your phone more than once an hour – if you've set it up right, it will alert you to anything you need to know without you having to check it between alerts.

So, don't keep your phone on your bedside table (or indeed even in the bedroom at nighttime) and resist the temptation to check it the moment you wake up. Buy an alarm clock to wake you up rather than using the alarm on your phone. Keep phones away from the table at mealtimes so you can chat with your family; the same when you're out socialising – interact with the people around you, there and then. Even when you're sitting watching television in the evening, don't be tempted to be on your phone as well – it's far better to engage fully in the programme or film.

You and your smartphone are like any healthy relationship – you need time away from each other.

Quickly…

• Make good use of your smartphone's diary and to-do list apps

• Set alerts for diary entries.

• Make use of repeating calendar and to-do entries for regular appointments and tasks.

• Share and sync your electronic calendar and to-do lists.

• Check emails on the go with your phone or tablet.

• Work from anywhere with a tablet or laptop.

• Use your phone or tablet for reading and much more.

• Don't let your smartphone intrude on your family life. Spend time 'unplugged'.

Chapter Six
Procrastinating

"The fear of death follows from the fear of life. A man who lives fully is prepared to die at any time"
  Mark Twain

I've been meaning to write about procrastination for a while but haven't managed to get around to it. Sorry, that's a feeble joke but the sentiment behind it will be all too familiar to many people – it certainly is to me. The truth is, procrastination is a massive time-waster – and for that, read life-waster.

My first memories of procrastination were when I was revising for my O Levels (yes, I really am that old), even if I didn't know it by that word back then. I knew what I had to do, but I'd begin by drawing up an elaborate revision timetable, all painstakingly colour-coded using my treasured pack of 30 felt-tip pens, then I would have to rearrange the items on my pinboard to make room for the timetable. Next, I'd notice that my textbooks were in a muddle, so I'd have to sort those into alphabetic, size or colour order, depending on which took my fancy that day. Finally, my desk would be a mess, so I'd clear everything off it, find that it was covered in dust, so I'd run downstairs for the Mr Sheen. Then, while I had the polish, I figured I might as well dust the entire bedroom, by which time my mum would be calling me down for dinner. It's just a good job I didn't have a computer keyboard to clean or a smartphone and social media to distract me back then.

Does that sound familiar? And I don't just mean from your school and university days, but right now? Do you ever put off jobs you don't want to do, or even those you do want to do, by finding distractions? Maybe completing that tax return, cleaning out the garage, starting that fitness routine, or writing that book. It's amazing how many other things you suddenly have to do when you really should be getting on with a task. Procrastination not only leads to stress when you end up with that last-minute panic to complete a job that you knew had to be done, but it also dashes countless dreams. How many people dreamed of writing a novel, climbing a mountain or travelling the world but never did it simply because they just couldn't quite get round to making a start? You are more likely to look back on your life and regret the things you didn't do, rather than the things you did. How annoying would it be to realise your life had passed by you and you'd never got around to doing that something you'd always promised yourself you'd do? There's no rewind button in life, so don't be one of though people who end up saying "If only…"

Making a start is the first step in doing anything, from cooking dinner to getting fit enough to run a marathon. Once you've made that first step, momentum kicks in, and you'll find yourself cracking on. How long does it take to make that first step? Well, that depends on what it is, but it's reasonable to say that two minutes of your valuable time is enough to leave the starting blocks and make some progress. And once you've committed to that first two minutes, the next two minutes will fly by and, before you know it, you've spent an hour doing something you either have to do or, more pleasantly, want to do.

Two minutes. My electric toothbrush has a timer that encourages me to clean my teeth for two minutes every morning and night, so I know what it feels like and I can assure you it's not very long. No one, and I mean no one, is so busy that they can't spare two minutes every once in a while. In procrastination terms, 120 seconds isn't even enough time to tidy your desk or clean your keyboard. Set a kitchen timer or your smartphone to two minutes and you'll see just how short a time it is.

The procrastinator's great excuses are, a) they have other things to do and so don't have the time and, b) it takes too long to get started. Lifesavers see it differently, so let's look at these one at a time:

Yes, we all have other things to do, but if you use the tips in this book to manage your time well, then you should surely be able to fit in just two minutes to kickstart something new. If it's something that has to be done and is hanging over you – such as that dreaded tax return – then the quicker you get on with it, the quicker it'll out of the way and you will feel so much better for completing it. On the other hand, if it's something you want to do, then it's even more important that you find time to start it.

I've said that two minutes is long enough to get started on something but when someone means it takes too long to get started, what they really mean is that the preamble takes too long. If that's the case, you need to use the two-minute rule again. If you want to take up oil painting, for instance, you have to buy brushes and canvases and maybe enrol on a course. The purchases can be made online in a matter of minutes, and a quick phone call or email will get you booked into a local class. Once you've done that, try to have somewhere in your home where an easel and paints can be left set up. That way, you don't have the excuse of having to get everything ready before you can paint. Being prepared in this way can help kickstart all sorts of things. Keep your gym bag packed so you can grab it and head to the gym without having to procrastinate while you dig out those shorts and trainers. Ensure your desk, whether at home or in the office, is always clear and tidy (and dusted!), so you can get straight to work without being tempted by a procrastinating and life-wasting spring clean, or be distracted by that magazine lying next to your keyboard, just teasing you to read it.

The trick here is to keep applying the two-minute rule – it's not a one-off cure-all. Devoting two minutes to starting a fitness campaign will certainly get that first session going but, the next day, you'll have to do the same two-minute kickstart, so ensure that your kit is all ready and tell yourself you only need to devote two minutes to getting going. Continue doing this for long enough and your daily exercise will become a routine that you will look forward to doing and you won't have to force yourself to get through that first two minutes to get going.

Getting fit, writing a novel or learning a new language, are examples of things we choose to do and, because of this, the two-minute rule is a great way of getting started and avoiding procrastination. However, there also plenty of things that we have to do but we put off because we're not looking forward to them. The aforementioned tax return, for instance. Often these are important tasks but we put them to the bottom of the pile because we simply can't face tackling them. And then, one day – towards the end of

January in the case of the tax return – we panic because the task has to be completed quickly. Something that was previously important has become urgent and, all of a sudden, we stop procrastinating and get on with the job in hand.

    While it's true that there is nothing like a deadline to focus the mind, leaving important jobs until they become urgent is not a good way to live your life. It leads to stress, panic, late nights and, most worrying, eats into time you could be spending doing something fun. So, if a task is important but not particularly enjoyable, schedule it in and get it done well in advance of it becoming urgent. Again, use the two-minute rule to make a start and it won't be as bad as you think – you'll soon be ticking it off your must-do list and feeling so much better for getting the difficult job out of the way. I like the saying 'eat the frog'. In other words, if you have an unpleasant task to do (such as eating a frog) then get it out of the way quickly rather than avoiding doing it. Try it now! Step away from this book, pick something from your list and take two minutes to do it.

    Once you've begun a task with a two-minute kickstart, it's important to stay focussed on it and not get distracted by other things. As a wise old sage possibly once said, think of a magnifying glass in the sun – move it around and nothing happens, but focus it on one point and you create fire. If you want to set your world alight, focus on one thing at a time. That, though, is easier said than done, especially with the distractions of the modern world. It's so easy to be working at a computer and lose your concentration in a moment when you hear that appealing ping of an incoming email, or your phone vibrates with a tempting text message.

While it's not realistic to avoid all distractions, you do need to minimise the risk of them happening while you are focussed on a task, and the good news is, that modern technology that causes distractions can also help you to avoid distractions. So, wherever possible, turn off email notifications on your computer and put your phone into do-not-disturb mode. It's also helpful to use your computer software in full-screen mode so there's nothing in the background, such as your Facebook feed or email program, to catch your eye. It's not just computer work that you need to focus on, even when you're doing something for fun, such as reading a book or watching a film, it's so easy to be distracted by your omnipresent mobile phone so, again, put it to sleep or, even better, leave it in another room. Checking emails, seeing what your friends are doing on Facebook and answering text messages are simply other forms of procrastination, so resist the temptation, stay focussed, and you'll get more done in less time.

So, what are you waiting for?

Quickly…
- You'll regret not getting on and doing things.
- Make a start on a task and momentum will kick in. Two minutes is enough to kickstart yourself
- Be prepared so you don't waste time getting ready to do something.
- Keep doing it every day.
- Don't leave important tasks until they become urgent or you'll panic.
- Focus on one thing at a time.
- Turn off and avoid distractions.

Chapter Seven
Boot the commute

"I've spent so many years commuting, I kind of prefer a home office"
   Hilary Clinton

As I explained in Chapter One, commuting – travelling long distances from home to your place of work – has become almost the norm for people in the UK and many other Western countries. Whether it's done by car, bus or train, commuting wastes valuable resources, creates congestion, eats into personal time, costs money and generally makes people miserable. Incidentally, the word commuter was coined back in the mid 19th century when Americans could pay a 'commuted' (reduced) rail fare into the cities where they worked.

The average commute to work and back in the UK takes 47 minutes and I bet a lot of people reading this will be thinking they wish their journey time was as short as that. However, even if 47 minutes doesn't sound much to you, that adds up to eight full days a year. That's over a week – you could take a lovely holiday abroad in that time. What's more, studies have shown that commuting is bad for your health; not only are there the obvious problems of stress and pollution, time wasted commuting means you have less time to spend on fitness and preparing meals. Next time you're at a railway station or motorway services, check out the amount of junk food people are eating; partly because they're not able to be at home making a proper meal.

John lives out in the country and has to travel 25 miles by car to his town-based job every day. "It doesn't sound far," he says, "but in the morning traffic, the journey takes me at least an hour. I tend to work late to avoid the evening rush hour but I'll still be lucky to get home within 45 minutes of leaving the office." One and three-quarter hours a day sitting in the car – that's over seven hours a week or nearly 16 days a year. Over a 40-year working life, John will spend almost two years commuting. Time he could have spent being more productive at his job or, even better, doing something he enjoys. He will also have driven 530,000 miles, used 15,000 gallons of petrol and spent untold amounts on the purchase, maintenance and depreciation of numerous cars. Some 76 percent of UK workers, outside of London, commute to work by car – no wonder there's so much congestion on the roads these days.

Often when people get to their offices, they sit at a computer all day, doing a job they could just as easily do at home. It's an outmoded system which is at odds with today's high-tech world where we are all so well interconnected. Telephones, emails, instant messaging, websites, shared productivity systems and video calling all combine to reduce the need for commuting for many workers and negate it altogether for some.

I'm realistic here and realise that it's not possible for, say, surgeons or teachers, to work from home. However, many jobs have a degree of admin involved – usually computer-based – so that work could be done at home, say one day a week, thus freeing up time and reducing the number of cars on the roads and people in trains. If one-third of commuters worked at home just one day a week, it would have a positive impact on congestion and the environment; not to mention workers' lives. In fact, many people could work from home more than one day, maybe heading into the office just one or two days a week.

At which point, people usually say something along the lines of: "Oh I couldn't possibly work from home, I'd sit and watch TV all day and wouldn't get anything done." In reality, though, home workers are more productive than those in offices. First of all, most daytime television isn't very good so the majority of most people would rather get on with something more interesting to keep boredom at bay. Second, if you're employed, you'll be keen to prove to your boss that, actually, you really can be trusted to spend a day or two working from home. Third, without the distractions of an office (colleagues chatting, phones ringing, bosses asking you to do things, trips to the coffee machine), you'll actually get more done at home. In fact, you'll probably find you'll be able to finish early and go off and do something fun.

If you really want to take control of your life, you'll want to kick out the daily commute altogether. And that means working closer to where you live or, even better, be based at home. Just imagine waking up in the morning and, instead of rushing out for the train and grabbing an over-hot coffee in a paper cup at the station, you get up at your own pace, relaxing over a freshly brewed coffee in a real cup as you nibble at a croissant, chatting to your family or catching up with the news on the television, radio or tablet. You shower and dress before going into your home office to start your working day, liaising with colleagues via email and video conferencing. And without constant interruptions throughout the day, you find you can get so much more done.

OK, that's not going to work for everyone, but at least try to live close by where you work, so it's only a short drive or, even better, a cycle ride or walk from your home. That way, you'll save time travelling and, if you can get there under your own power, you'll improve your health and do your bit for the environment as well. If you think that's not feasible, consider John's story. He admits himself he could leave his village home and move to the market town where he works. "It's a lovely place and, now the children have grown up, my wife and I would enjoy being closer to restaurants and the theatre. I could walk to work and to the shops, and property is cheaper, too. What's more, the money I'd be saving in travel costs, I could put toward my dream sports car, which would only get used on the weekends. Driving would become fun again."

An alternative to moving closer to your place of work is to do the opposite and find a job closer to your home. OK, this may mean taking a pay cut (but how much money do you actually need – see Chapter Eight). However, if you factor in the cost of travelling – in terms of money, time and stress – it can make a lot of sense. Accountant Rachel did just that: "I was living in Brighton and working in London for a large accountancy practice. The money was good, ridiculously good, but I hated the crowded train journey up to London and back every day. People say you can work on the train, but you will struggle to do so during rush hour, when you're lucky to get a seat."

Rachel did some sums and worked out she was spending a whopping £5000 a year in train fares alone, plus wasting over 500 hours travelling – that's 20 days a year sitting (or, more likely, standing) in a crowded train. "I asked myself if the stress and expense was worth it, and knew immediately it wasn't. Brighton is a thriving city and I soon found a job with a local accountancy firm. OK, I had to take a £10,000 pay cut, but I can now cycle to work, which has helped me to lose some weight, which is great. What's more, the team of people I'm working with are so much friendlier and more relaxed than those I was with in London. I'm sure that's because they don't have the stress of commuting and live in a wonderful place.

The ideal scenario is to work from home, so you don't need to travel any distance to an office at all. This means you are not contributing at all to pollution or congestion and free up valuable time that you can spend doing what you want to do. Plus you will save money that would otherwise be spent on trains, buses, fuel or car maintenance, which means you don't need to earn as much, or you can put that money towards something you really want to spend it on.

I've yet to speak to anyone who enjoys commuting; it eats into their time, it's stressful, uncomfortable, boring, lonely and depressing. And yet people continue to do it. You may point out that it's unlikely that we are going to kill off commuting anytime soon – it's just too ingrained into western society, and our towns and cities have developed to embrace a commuting way of life. That may be so, but it's no reason for you personally not to take a stand and adopt a more pleasant and responsible lifestyle. Even if other people don't.

Quickly…
- Commuting wastes time and resources.
- Working from home at least one day a week frees up time and reduces congestion.
- Home workers are more productive than those in offices.
- Live close to your place of work.
- Commuting won't go away but you can choose not to.

Chapter Eight
How much money do you need?

"Life is what happens while you are busy making other plans"
John Lennon

Many very wealthy people are fond of saying that they only got to where they are today by working 25 hours a day, eight days a week (yes, I'm sure some of them really do exaggerate). That's fine if you enjoy it; I know a top surgeon who is rarely home before 10pm at night, but he says he loves every minute of his highly-paid work because he gets immense satisfaction from helping his patients overcome illness. And thank goodness there are people like that in the world. For him, the money is secondary to his healing skills and the immense sense of achievement he gets from his work. On the other hand, is it right to work long hours simply to amass great wealth? Well, yes, it is if you enjoy doing that, as the Alan Sugars and Richard Bransons of this world obviously do, and who are we to knock them?

On the other hand, what if you are working long hours earning lots of money but you don't particularly enjoy your job? If that's the case, then maybe it's time to step back and reassess what is really important to you. Sure, money can give you a very nice lifestyle but it's not going to be at all pleasant if you're too stressed with work to enjoy your hard-earned luxuries, never mind enjoying your family and friends. If this is the case for you, perhaps you need to cut back on the spending and lead a simpler life, which will remove the pressure to have to earn so much money and, in turn, that will give you more free time to do what you enjoy.

But, you may point out, you like having a smart car, exotic holidays and beautiful clothes. That's fine but maybe you can have a similar lifestyle for less outlay. Oh, and if you're not in the category of earning lots of money, this chapter will also help you to live better and maybe even cut down your expenses enough to work part-time.

Sounds too good to be true? It's not; read on to find out how to have the finer things in life without needing a lot of money.

Let's start with cars – something close to my heart with my Porsche sales business. I'm always astonished at the number of people who buy brand new cars on finance. That's a surefire way of wasting money, as a typical new car will lose 40 percent of its value in the first year and 60 percent over the first three years of its life; not smart when you also add in the cost of borrowing the money to buy the thing in the first place. A typical £20,000 new family car will cost you well over £30,000 when you factor in depreciation and interest on a loan.

It makes far more sense, then, to buy a car that's three years old or more in the first place. You'll pay 60 percent less for it and not have to borrow as much, if any, money for it. That £20,000 car has now cost you only around £8000! And don't think that an older car will be unreliable – modern cars just keep going and there's no reason why one won't still be smart and reliable even after ten years of average use. If you're in the UK and are really that worried about what the neighbours will say if your car doesn't boast latest age-related plate, then spend a few hundred pounds on a personal plate which will hide the age of the car and impress your shallow-minded neighbours at the same time. What's more, buying a used car will also allow you to buy a better model than if you opted for a brand-new one. My grandmother used to say that newness is a novelty that wears off – wise words from a wise woman.

I get a lot of customers coming to me saying that they've always wanted a Porsche and now they've reached a stage in their lives when they can make that dream come true; usually the kids have left home and the mortgage has been paid off. They're very excited about this and I love to help people realise their dreams. By the way, I'm talking about Porsches here because that's what I know, but the same principle will apply to other cars. In recent years, classic Porsche 911 values have shot up as people have been buying them as investments (with interest rates low, classic cars are better than cash in the bank), but they remain good value for money and a safe buy because they will at least hold their value and, if you're lucky, will appreciate. So you can drive a cool car without losing money. Fantastic!

As wonderful as classic 911s are, some people prefer the convenience and sophistication of more modern cars. And while a brand-new 911 starts at around £75,000 and goes up to about £150,000, you can live the dream for much, much less. Reasonable modern Porsche 911s start at around £13,000, while £20,000 will get you something seriously good – put that private plate on it and it'll look a million dollars. It's not just 911s, either; many people dream of cruising around in an open-top sports car when they retire but why wait when you can get a decent Porsche Boxster today for as little as £7000? On the other hand, perhaps you're more of a 4x4 type of person, in which case a big Porsche Cayenne can be picked up for under £10,000. Sure, the running costs of a Porsche are going to be a bit higher than for a new Ford Fiesta but there are plenty of independent specialists out there who offer servicing and parts for sensible money. And, crucially, a modern Porsche bought at these levels is going to lose little, if anything, in value during your ownership. Besides, once you've read Chapter Seven, you'll be cutting down the number of miles you drive, anyway.

Speaking of ownership, how often do you change your car and how much do you lose each time you trade one in for another? Many years ago, I read a book called Sustainable Car Ownership which showed how it made sense to keep the same car for many years, repairing it when it went wrong rather than sending it to the scrapheap. You wouldn't throw your house away when it needed a new boiler, so why write-off your car just because the clutch is gone? OK, you have to weigh up the financial considerations before pouring good money into a car that has little residual value but there is a lot of sense in not swapping cars every two or three years.

A car is something that most of us need throughout our lives but what about those things we dream of owning in retirement? I live on England's south coast where there are some great places to sail so, naturally, a lot of my friends dream of having a yacht when they finish work. However, once you're in your sixties, you may not have many years left to enjoy a boat and, more importantly, you may not have the money to keep one. Around here, you're looking at around £5000 a year to keep a typical 30-foot yacht on a marina berth, although one way to cut that figure right down is to keep the boat on a mooring instead.

Visit a boat show and look at the luxury yachts on display and you'd be forgiven that thinking that sailing is a rich person's sport. It can be, course, but it doesn't have to be, as Mike explains: "I looked at various ways of buying a brand-new but fairly average 30-foot yacht for around £100,000 but I just couldn't make the figures add up, with the costs of finance and depreciation scaring me.

"Then I started looking at secondhand boats and found myself a lovely 32-foot sailing yacht. She was up for sale at £25,000 but the owner just couldn't shift her and didn't want to continue paying to keep her on the marina, so I haggled with him and bought the yacht for just £20,000. She was built in the 1980s and, while structurally sound, was looking a bit tired inside and out. I spent a year doing the boat up in my spare time, which I thoroughly enjoyed, as did my teenage son, as it gave us a shared interest and we really bonded over the work. I probably spent an additional £5000 on new fittings and materials spread comfortably over that period but we now have a lovely yacht that really feels as if she has part of my son and me in her. I could easily sell her today for more than £25,000 if I wanted to. I won't, though, as I plan to enjoy using her for the next 20 years or so, including doing my dream sail around Britain."

Not into sailing? No problem, this same philosophy can be used to buy today other things you've alway dreamed of having in retirement. One big craze for retirees at the moment is to own a motorhome and, again, these are serious money new, with prices starting at around £70,000. Browse AutoTrader, though, and you can find a respectable used one for £20,000 which won't make you look like a new-age traveller. You may need to invest in some new cushions and curtains but then you'll be ready to hit the road.

OK, maybe a nomadic lifestyle isn't your idea of a great holiday, but you can enjoy visiting exotic countries without having to spend a fortune. Sure, five-star hotels are nice but, at the end of the day, a hotel is really just somewhere to sleep – a more modest establishment can be just as comfortable for half the price, while a bed-and-breakfast or hostel will be even cheaper and can immerse you in the local culture. Shop around for late deals online and try to be flexible about where you go and when you go, and there are some huge savings to be had. Also, you don't have to go on an expensive long-haul flight to have a great holiday. If you live in Europe, there's a huge variety of scenery, culture and weather on your doorstep, with most countries within a three-hour flight from you.

Even better, don't even leave the country – here in the UK we have a wealth of wonderful places to visit and many of us haven't even scratched the surface of what's on offer. The same can be said of other countries, too.

Sandra found this when planning an ultimate family getaway. "Our twin sons were about to leave for university so we thought it would be good to have a last holiday that we'd all remember. The boys wanted to go to California, which would have been wonderful but the £12,000 price tag made it a no-go – the long-haul flights were a big chunk of that. Instead, we hired a large motorhome and cruised down through France, Switzerland and Italy for two weeks. We had a brilliant time, discovered some beautiful places, ate some delicious food and really bonded as a family. It cost less than half as much as the USA trip would have been and we all agreed we came away with some fantastic memories. Plus, we've plenty of money left over for a family skiing trip in the winter – so much for that final holiday!"

Graham, on the other hand, no longer takes holidays, arguing that his lifestyle doesn't demand them. "A holiday is a break but I don't need a break from my everyday life because it's not stressful and I enjoy my work." He makes an interesting point that ties in with the history lesson in Chapter One. Holidays are a relatively recent invention that gave factory workers a temporary escape from their toil. Today, they do much the same thing for many unhappy employees. However, if you have a proper work/leisure balance (remember we don't talk about work/life), then you should have no need to get away from it all. Graham says that's just how he feels: "I live in Cornwall where I spend my time surfing and mountain biking. The weather is reasonable, the scenery is great and I can do everything I want here, so why go anywhere else? Every day is a holiday for me!" What a great lifesaving philosophy to have but some people do like to travel and discover new places and, if that's you, then it's important that you create a life that allows you to do that. You shouldn't have to put off travelling until retirement.

Again, this is possible without having a holiday in the traditional fortnight in the summer sense, as Maria has found: "I run a collection of online blogs which generate a useful income for me," she explains. "I do everything from my iPad – I dumped the laptop last year as I didn't need it – so can work from anywhere in the world, which is exactly what I do. I've rented out my London flat, which itself gives me a useful extra income, and have spent the last six months in New Zealand and Australia, travelling around, visiting friends and having fun. One of the great things about travelling, is that there is plenty of downtime hanging around at airports and stations, and sitting on planes and trains – time which I put to good use working on my blogs. As I do this, I look around at the bored faces around me and wonder why they're not doing the same, then they'd free up time later to enjoy themselves. Life should be a holiday, not a chore!"

Going back to our original question of how much money do you actually need, while I don't suggest you live like a monk (although if you really want to, then I'd admire you for doing so) but how much 'stuff' do you require in your life? Increasingly in western society, people feel the need to accumulate more and more possessions – consumerism has become almost a religion, with huge and opulent shopping malls being the new cathedrals. People shop to attain happiness but, sadly, it rarely works. Sure, it's good to have nice things and, if a new pair of shoes makes you happy, then, by all means, treat yourself. The lifesaver's key, though, is not to take it to excess – ten new pairs of shoes is not going to make you ten times happier than one pair. Just buy what you need, with the occasional treats thrown in from time to time – and only when you can afford it. Look back to the 1950s and it's astonishing to see how few possessions the typical UK family owned. In the mid-1950s, only eight percent of British households owned a fridge – something which is considered an essential today. Ten years after that, just 20 percent of homes had a telephone, while today there are more mobile phones than people in the UK. I remember travelling to Sri Lanka a few years ago and the flight stopped off at Abu Dhabi, the capital of the oil-rich United Arab Emirates. Walking around the glittering airport there, the opulence was almost obscene, with shops selling gold watches, jewellery for eye-watering prices. By comparison, the duty-free shops at Columbo airport in Sri Lanka were selling washing machines – a very different idea of luxury.

Live modestly and you'll live happily, as Lisa discovered: "When I left university and started working I had, for the first time in my life, some spare money so I went mad every weekend buying clothes. I can't deny I enjoyed myself but, after a few months, I realised that I'd maxed out on my credit cards and store cards, while my wardrobe was full of clothes I hardly wore, as I preferred to stick with a few favourite items. Something had to change, so I cut up the cards and set up a programme to pay off my debts. It took a year of frugal living but, you know what, it did me good. I realised that, actually, I didn't need all that stuff cluttering up my life. Now I still enjoy shopping for clothes – hey, I'm a girl! – but only when I really want or need something. The money I'm saving I use for holidays, plus I've managed to buy my first house, so the future's looking good."

Lisa is lucky in that she realised early on where she was going wrong and was able to nip her spending in the bud. Others, though, have got themselves into serious trouble with excessive spending, and have ended up having to work even more to feed their addiction – not the route to happiness they'd hoped for. Getting into debt and becoming a slave to your credit card is not the way forward. Living within your means and not borrowing money is.

Cutting down on spending not only saves you money, but it also simplifies your life. All those clothes Lisa was buying were cluttering up her home. Look around at the 'stuff' you own. Do you need it all? If not, have a clear out, sell some stuff on eBay or at a car boot sale. Your home – and therefore you – will then be more relaxed. Also, if we all consumed less, we'd put fewer demands on the world's stretched resources which, in the long term, will benefit all of us.

Speaking of which, things have become disposable. I remember when I was a boy in the 1970s, my father would mend things. If the kettle or toaster stopped working, he'd fit a new element. Today, though, we're more likely to throw out a broken appliance and buy a new one because products are often so cheap and we have more disposable income. Yet the internet (something my dad never had to help him) makes it so much easier to repair things, with parts available mail-order and websites and videos showing you how to fix everything from washing machines to laptops. Not only can doing this save you money and reduce environmental waste, but it's also immensely satisfying to be able to fix something.

It's not just physical stuff which we can get bogged down with, either. Are you cluttering up your life with too much activity? It's a bane of modern life that we always seem to be rushing around, doing things that are meant to be enjoyable. "This hit home to me one Saturday a couple of years ago," remembers Jason. "I went for a bike ride in the afternoon then had to rush back to head off to friends for a barbecue, but I needed to go home via the supermarket to pick up some beers to take along, and also fit in time for a quick – and, it has to be said, much-needed – shower. Two supposedly pleasurable events became a stress because time was against me. What I should have done was buy the beers the evening before, and set off earlier for my cycle rather going shopping with my girlfriend that morning. In addition, at that time, I was going to the gym three times a week, playing five-a-side football every Wednesday evening, meeting up with my cycling mates most Fridays for a few beers, and at the same time holding down a full-time job and trying to spend quality time with my girlfriend."

Jason decided something had to give so he could enjoy, well, enjoying himself. "I cut the gym down to once a week unless I had some spare time, in which case I'd pop in for an extra session or two. I also got out of the habit of the Friday nights with the cycling mates and now just catch up with them very occasionally on Fridays but, more regularly, on our weekend rides which, after all, is what cycling friends are all about!"

Minimalism is good in terms of architecture, technology and art, so why not our lives? Simplify everything, from the amount of stuff you own, to the amount of things you do and the amount of think about, and your life will be easier and less stressful.

Also, before you buy anything new, wait a while rather than making an impulse purchase. After a week or two, that new blouse or gadget you felt you just had to have may not seem quite as essential as you thought it was. We've all done this – bought something on impulse and then regretted it – the nation's cupboards, drawers and garages are full of discarded purchases. Hold fire before you buy and you could end up saving yourself money and have a less cluttered home.

A final thought: rather than yearning after buying the next 'thing' in your life, be it a new car, a pair of shoes or the latest gadget, just look at what you already have and be grateful for that. After all, you have much more than most of the world's population. Turn to Chapter Eleven for more about being grateful for what you have already.

Quickly...

- If you're not enjoying working hard to maintain a lifestyle, it's time to cut back on your spending.
- You can have nice cars, holidays and the like without a big outlay.
- Buy used rather than new, and repair rather than replace.
- If you enjoy your work you don't need to take holidays.
- Only buy what you need and wait before you splash out.
- Cut down on your activities as well as your spending. Less is more.
- Be grateful for what you already have.

Chapter Nine
Health is the best wealth

"Physical fitness is not only one of the most important keys to a healthy body, it is the basis of dynamic and creative intellectual activity"
John F. Kennedy

The whole purpose of this book is to show you ways to make the most of the short time you have on this planet and, while there's no guarantee of a long, happy life, there are ways to stack the odds in your favour. The best way to do this is to keep fit and healthy. What's more, if you adopt some of the ideas in this book, you will free up time to spend keeping fit which, in turn, will give you more energy, vitality and motivation to get even more done and so free up even more time. A brilliant win-win lifesaving situation!

There is, though, a danger in keeping fit – you can spend an awful lot of time obsessing over what you eat, how much you eat, and what sort of exercise you do. If you enjoy cooking and eating super-healthily then that's just fine, and by all means, spend your spare time doing just that. The same goes for fitness – if you're a dedicated bodybuilder or get a kick out of Ironman events, then it's important to make time to hone a perfect body. On the other hand, you may just want to be reasonably fit and healthy. With all the publicity about healthy eating at the moment, some people get obsessed about what they put into their bodies, to the extent it makes them mentally unwell – a condition called Orthorexia Nervosa. Sufferers check every ingredient of every food they consume and panic if they have to eat anything which they're not entirely sure what it contains. If it doesn't precisely fit that week's fad diet, it's a strict no-no.

The media bombards us with information about what is good or bad for us and it's extremely confusing for anyone hoping to be healthy. I remember not too many years ago the advice was to eat no more than three eggs a week, but now we're told that eggs are super-foods and three a day is great. Is red wine good or bad? Should we eat red meat or not? Brown rice used to be good but is it today? Who knows? The advice seems to change almost daily, and the reality is no one really knows what a healthy diet it. Some people advocate eating only what our Palaeolithic ancestors consumed – fruit, nuts and meat, basically – and to avoid grains and sugars, while others insist that brown rice and bread is the way forward. There's even an argument for concentrating on foods which are super-high in fat. No wonder people get ill worrying about what to eat.

And that's no good if we are hoping to enjoy life to the full and have time to spend doing what we really want. So what's the answer? Well, the old adage 'anything in moderation' is a good starting point, although you'll perhaps not be surprised to read that some people say that this advice will send you to any early grave. However, in the absence of any better suggestions (or at least ones that aren't going to go out of favour in a few months), I reckon it's the best way forward. Essentially, then, if you like an occasional cream bun, bar of chocolate or pint of beer, then, by all means, go ahead and enjoy one – the key words here being 'occasional' and 'one'. We all know that cakes, chocolate and alcohol aren't good for you (or are they?) so it's sensible to consume such things in moderation. But what of all those other foods which so-called experts don't seem to be able to decide on? Meat, fruit, grains, dairy products and, indeed, pretty much every foodstuff you can think of? Well, again, don't overdo any of them and ensure you have a balanced diet. Thanks to rationing and the government encouraging people to turn their gardens into allotments, the British ate surprisingly healthily during the Second World War – freshly grown vegetables, not too much meat, fat or sugar, and, crucially, smallish portions. I'm not suggesting going back to Spam fritters and dried egg, but the wartime diet showed that avoiding anything in excess – including the amount of food consumed – is a good thing. So, don't get hung up on fad diets, just eat sensibly.

The other crucial thing about your health is to balance what goes in with what goes out. No, don't worry, I'm not talking about bodily functions, but rather the number of calories you burn. Rather like as a car burns fuel to run, your body burns food to function, and a calorie is a unit of energy. The more calories you put into your body, the more you have to use up to maintain an equilibrium, and the problem is any calories you don't burn, tend to remain in your body in the form of fat. The idea being that the body doesn't like to waste food in case there's a shortage in the future, so it stores it as fat. So that spare tyre around your waist is the human equivalent of a camel's hump and would have been handy in prehistoric times when food would be hard to find during the winter, but less so when there's a Waitrose just around the corner. A typical adult male consumes around 2500 calories a day and, the good news is, he will burn a good chunk of that off by just being alive – the human body is a complex device and requires a lot of power to keep going (a number of calories you burn like this is called the Basal Metabolic Rate or BMR). The problem occurs when the body doesn't burn all the calories that go in – if 2500 are consumed but only 2000 are burned, that excess 500 calories can lead to a person gaining weight at around half a kilo a week – that's half a bag of sugar. On the other hand, if you burn the same amount as you put in, your weight should remain constant.

Once again, there's a danger here of becoming obsessed with calories, which can be time-consuming and cause you stress, and that's not what we want. It is, though, a good idea to get a sense of how many calories you are taking in and using up. Thankfully, technology is our friend here, as William found out: "As I hit 50, I realised that I was getting a bit podgy and not as fit as I used to be. Middle-age, too much good food and an office job were taking their tool, so I decided that I had to take action," explains the solicitor. "However, I didn't have the time nor inclination to get too anal about diet and exercise. So I simply took control of my eating and went for smaller portions and cut down on sugar, fat and alcohol, which was easy enough for me to do and seemed a logical first step to losing weight."

William then turned to his smartphone for help: "I downloaded an app called MyFitnessPal. This allowed me to track the number of calories I was consuming, simply by entering the details of each meal I ate. I have to admit, it was a bit of a pain to do this for every meal of every day, so I just kept it up for a month, after which I knew that my average daily consumption was 2000 calories. Some days were lower and others were higher, but that average figure was good enough for me to work with."

His next task was to work out how many calories he was burning, and William began with his Basal Metabolic Rate (or BMR, the number of calories his body uses just being alive). This can be calculated by using the formula "10 x weight (kg) + 6.25 x height (cm) − 5 x age (years) + "5 or, as William found out, his iPhone's Health app sorts it out for you once you've inputted your vital statistics (other health apps do the same thing, or there are online BMR calculators). "My BMR is 1500 which means that I burn 1500 calories without even moving, so I need to get through an extra 500 active calories a day to maintain equilibrium," he explains.

How do you know how many active calories a day you burn? Today, there is a range of gadgets available to help. William opted for an Apple Watch which tracks activity and heart rate to give a pretty accurate account of active calories: "I was pleased to find that, even on a relatively sedentary day in the office, I would get through around 250 calories, when I wasn't doing much activity. With that in mind, I set the Watch's daily goal to 500 active calories and that has encouraged me to move around more. I stand up and stroll around the office while I'm on the phone, use any excuse to run up and down the stairs, get off the Tube a stop early and walk the remaining distance home, and generally make myself more active. The Watch even reminds me to stand up if it senses I've been sitting for an hour. Sometimes it's a struggle to hit 500 active calories, but I also go to the gym twice a week and each time that adds an extra 1000 calories to my daily score; about the same as a weekend bike ride. And when I have done that extra exercise, I don't feel too guilty about having an occasional pint of beer in the evening!"

Our friend William has a good strategy in that he can live a relatively fit lifestyle without getting obsessed with what he eats or, indeed, does. He uses his Apple Watch to help him achieve his daily fitness goals and is sensible about his food intake. I'm also an Apple Watch fan and use mine in very much the same way; to help maintain my weight and health. It works well for me because I respond well to targets – the Watch not only monitors my active calories burned, but also encourages me to spend 30 minutes a day in exercise and to stand and walk around for at least one minute every hour. For me, working towards those goals each day is a great motivator and I always aim to hit them, even when I'm not doing any form of sport. On the days I go to the gym or out on my bike, I treat the extra calories burned as additional to my standard 600 I have to reach, rather than part of them.

While standing, walking and taking the stairs will all make a worthwhile difference to your health and wellbeing, you also need to spend at least a couple of hours a week doing more vigorous exercise – the sort of stuff that will get you a bit out of breath and, more importantly, raise your heart rate. Your heart is a muscle and, as such, needs exercise to keep it in good condition, and the way to do that is to encourage it to pump more blood around your body. Once again, technology, such as the Apple Watch, will measure your heart rate and show you when you're getting it working hard but there's an easier way of knowing when your heart is pumping fast. First of all, you'll be able to feel it thumping away and, second, there's a handy correlation between heart rate and breathlessness. If you've just cycled up a steep hill and are out of breath at the top, you'll know that your heart will also be pumping sixteen to the dozen. As you get fitter, your heart will become stronger and won't have to beat as fast to pump the same amount of blood around your body as you exercise, and when you are at rest, your heart beat will be slower. A typical adult will have a resting heart rate of around 60 beats per minute, while that figure can drop as low as 40 in the case of super-fit athletes. I get my vigorous exercise from gym sessions, cycling and sailing, so discover your passion and start working out.

If an Apple Watch is not for you, there is a range of fitness bands available that do much the same job in encouraging you to be active and hit goals, and even your smartphone in your pocket will have a pretty good stab of keeping track of your movement. And if that's all too high tech for you, then simply aim to be active for at least 30 minutes a day and, if you have a desk-bound job, make sure you get out of your seat every hour for a few moments.

Remember, this isn't an exact science at this level. Unless you are using laboratory test equipment, you are never going to know precisely how many calories you are burning, as there are just so many variables that consumer products can't allow for, and the relationship between food intake and calories burned is somewhat more complex than I'm making it out to be. However, that doesn't matter so long as you are making an effort to be active and eat sensibly, and products such as an Apple Watch will help by encouraging you to keep reasonably active every day.

Going to the gym or partaking in some form of sport or organised exercise isn't for everyone. Indeed, some people argue that it's a waste of their precious time. Andrew is one such person: "I hate the idea of sport or any form of dedicated exercise but I do want to keep fit and healthy," he says. Andrew's solution is to ensure he has a healthy lifestyle and keeps fit going about his day: "On a typical day, I cycle to school with my kids," he explains. "Then I continue to work on my bike – it's only a ten-mile ride, which I do all year round regardless of the weather. Then, at the weekends, I spend time on my allotment. I love doing this, it keeps me active, gets me outdoors and it has the bonus of providing my family and me with healthy, organic food." This is a clever lifestyle for Andrew; he keeps fit without having to dedicate time to or invest in expensive gym memberships. There's nothing new about Andrew's lifestyle – by growing his own food and getting to work under his own steam, he's doing just what most people did until relatively recently.

If being fit sounds like too much hassle for you, just remember that being moderately obese can reduce your life expectancy by five years, while if you are severely obese, you can say goodbye to ten years. That's as bad as spending a lifetime smoking. Furthermore, for people in their 50s and 60s, just 30 minutes of exercise every day can reduce the risk of a heart attack by 50 percent, and can reduce the effects of ageing. If all that doesn't get you off the couch, then nothing will!

Health isn't just about your physical body, either. It's also down to mental attitude. How often do you hear people say "Ooh, I'm getting old, I can't do that anymore"? Tell yourself that and, guess what, your mind and body will believe it's true. Mark is in his forties and insists he'll never be able to ski because he has 'bad knees'. He's never had them checked by a doctor, he just says this and has resigned himself to, what in his mind, is a fact. Glynn, on the other hand, is 72 and, despite X-rays showing her knees are showing signs of wear, skis every year and is even planning to learn to snowboard. "I'm not old and refuse to give into trivial niggles," she insists. So next time you're about to moan about your joints, your eyesight, a lingering cold, or your health in general, take a moment and, instead, say to yourself with a smile: "I'm fit and healthy." Do this enough, and your mind and body will, remarkably, start to believe it and you will feel so much better in yourself.

The above relates to people who are already reasonably fit and well. If you have any concerns about your health, do consult a medical professional before embarking on a fitness routine. Neither will these simple tips bring you to marathon-running fitness but, on the other hand, if you simply want to lead a healthier – and possibly longer – life than they will certainly do that without impacting too much on your time.

Quickly...
- Don't waste time obsessing about health and diet.
- Eat a sensible and balanced diet.
- Over a month, measure the calories you consume.
- Work out your Basal Metabolic Rate: the amount of calories you burn just being alive.
- The difference between the calories you consume and burn determines the amount of exercise you need to do.

- A fitness tracker will help you maintain a healthy lifestyle.
- Mental attitude has an impact on your fitness. You're as old as you feel.

Chapter Ten
It's good to be selfish, sometimes

"Don't sacrifice yourself too much, because if you sacrifice too much there's nothing else you can give and nobody will care for you"
　Karl Lagerfeld

We've all been called selfish at some point in our lives and, invariably, it will have been a negative comment about our behaviour. The child who scoffs all the sweets without sharing them with their friends, the teenager who never does anything to help around the house, the thief who steals from a pensioner, the mother who neglects her children to go drinking. All examples of selfish behaviour. Society tells us that it's bad to put ourselves before other people and we should always sacrifice ourselves for others.

Not always, though. Every time you travel on an aeroplane, you're told to be selfish – 'in case of an emergency, fit your own face mask before helping others with theirs'. And that is a good metaphor for why it can be good to be selfish – look after yourself and you'll be in a stronger position to help others.

If you take the time to be fit and healthy, by eating the right foods and exercising regularly, you'll be physically and emotionally stronger to care for your family, and you may well live longer, giving them more years with you. There's also less chance of you developing a long-term illness that would demand relatives having to care for you.

In today's world, it's all too easy to spend all your time doing things for others and neglecting your own desires and well-being. Keeping a boss, partner, children and even parents happy can leave very little time for you. And that's not healthy for anyone.

Samantha discovered this as she juggled work and family: "I'm a primary school teacher so have a busy time, not only teaching, but also caring for my pupils' wellbeing and dealing with their problems. These may seem minor, but in their world, it's a major thing when, say, an eight-year old's best friend tells her she hates her. I'm married with two great teenage children and a husband who is busy running his own business, so when I get home from school, I have meals to cook, washing to do, a house to clean and be a taxi driver to the kids. On top of all that, my parents are getting on a bit and struggle with day-to-day things, so I do shopping for them, helping with their housework and, if

I have time, take them out in the car to give them a change of scene. It became so normal that I didn't realise I wasn't happy until my son told me that I was always snappy and grumpy. I said he was a fine one to talk but, after, I thought about his words and realised that he was right. I wasn't a nice person to be with and, rushing around trying to keep everyone happy meant that, bizarrely, I wasn't having any quality time with any of them. What's more, my own hobbies of jogging and playing the piano had completely taken a back seat."

It all came to a head one night when Samantha broke down in tears and told her husband all about the stresses of her life. "Dave was wonderfully understanding," she smiles. "He admitted that I'd been grumpy and withdrawn but thought it was an age thing! We sat down together and drew up an action plan to free up some time for me to do what I wanted. That included the children being left to cook their own meals a couple of times a week, so that was less for me to do. Dave then contacted social services and found out that my parents qualified for help with their cleaning and meals, which meant that, when I did visit them we could concentrate on doing enjoyable things."

Samantha, with the help of her husband, who admits to being super-organised at work, managed to free up enough time for her to go jogging at least three times a week, take piano lessons every Wednesday evening and play for 30 minutes a day, plus spend more quality time with her fast-growing teenagers while they were still at home. "I used to feel bad doing things for myself," admits Samantha, "but I now realise that it's essential to have some me-time in my life. I feel fitter, less stressed, happier and, my family tell me, a nicer person to be with."

What Samantha has discovered is that to be a well-rounded member of society, you need to have a balance between thinking of others and thinking of yourself. It has been suggested that selfish behaviour is a survival instinct which dates back to prehistoric times – if you were being chased by a wild animal, you'd do your best to escape without worrying about your fellow men. As we learned to live in communities, though, it became more necessary to work as a team and think of others. Which does make sense, and an essential cornerstone of civilisation. At the same time, however, you have to be a little bit selfish from time to time, so long as it's not the sort of negative behaviour that hurts others – share those sweets!

The bad sort of selfishness can be thought of as being self-centred – the kind of conduct that puts your needs first without any consideration as to how your actions will affect others. Mugging an old lady for her pension money, hogging a seat on a train when a less-able person is standing, letting a colleague take the rap for a mistake which was actually your fault, always putting yourself first, regardless, are all examples of bad selfishness.

On the other hand, good selfishness is being self-focused for part of each day. Making time to do what you want, rather than devoting all your time to others. Saying no to working late because you want to go to the gym. Telling your kids you're all having the healthy salad you want for dinner instead of the pizza they're demanding. Explaining to your wife that, just this once, she'll be home alone next Friday night because you're catching up with your old university mates for the first time in years.

Not only does good selfishness enable you to sometimes do what you want to do, there's also evidence that it's good for you not to spend all your time trying to please other people; you can end up getting addicted to the buzz of receiving gratitude from others and become unable to be happy without that approval. In effect, you can lose your individuality which isn't good for your relationships with family, friends and colleagues, not to mention your relationship with yourself. So, being selfish can actually make you less selfish!

At this point, you may well be feeling uncomfortable at the thought of being selfish, but that's because the word has such negative connotations. How about using the phrase 'me-time' instead, which has a cosier, friendlier ring to it? Use your diary (see Chapter Three) to ensure that you schedule in some me-time every day, and you'll feel a lot better about the idea of being selfish.

Quickly…
- Put yourself first sometimes.
- Ask for help if you find yourself spending all your time doing things for other people.
- Plan your days to give you some me-time.
- Bad selfishness doesn't help you or others.
- Good selfishness is essential to give you a balanced life.

Chapter Eleven
Don't worry, about a thing

"I've had a lot of worries in my life, most of which never happened"
Mark Twain

Like many quotes attributed to the great man, the one above may or may not have been said by Mark Twain, but there's a lot of truth in it. In fact, a study showed that 85 percent of issues people get worked up about never actually materialise. And of the remaining 15 percent that do happen, 79 percent of the people questioned said that, in fact, they coped with the problem better than anticipated, and some even came away from the experience having learned something worthwhile. To save you doing the maths, all this means that a full 97 percent of what you fret over isn't worth, well, fretting over. So what a complete waste of time worrying is!

Worry is not only a time-waster – and the point of this book is to help you stop wasting time – it also leads to stress, which can make you unwell and even shorten your existence – which, again, is contrary to what this book is about, and what lifesavers want from their lives.

It is very easy to say "don't worry", and it's highly likely that people say it to you regularly, and you probably tell other people: "Oh, don't worry, it'll be fine". It is one of the commonest things we say when someone is fretting about something. It's probably one of the most ignored bits of advice, too. You start off with a nagging thought and, before you know it, you've blown it out of all proportion and are getting stressed out over something which you simply can't get out of your mind. So how do you stop worrying about things?

Worry, as Mark Twain is claimed to have implied, is when you overthink about something that has yet to happen, might happen, and if it does happen, is rarely as bad as you expect. Think back over things you have worried about during your life: your first day at a new school or a new job, your wedding day, a dental appointment, a sporting event, or a conflict with a friend or colleague. I can guarantee that you'll remember that, when they actually happened, all those things went far better than you expected. In fact, you probably enjoyed them (well, maybe not the dental appointment). So next time you start worrying about something (and it probably won't be long before you do) then just think back to a similar scenario and remember how that turned out in the end.

You can go one stage further and visualise in your mind just how well this particular concern is going to pan out, based on your past experiences. You can't visualise? Well, if you can worry, you certainly can visualise. Worrying is playing through worst-case scenarios in your mind, imagining just what could – and will – go wrong and how awful things will be. How about, then, you use that powerful imagination to turn things around and visualise just how good things will be? You could call it positive worrying!

This is an astonishingly powerful strategy: all that mental energy you've spent imagining the worst can be turned around to visualising the best. And, guess what, doing that is far less stressful, more enjoyable and will make your life so much more pleasant. You may even find some of the positive things you imagine will actually come true.

Matt is a salesman who used to worry constantly about meeting with potential new clients: "I'd get really worked up as I was driving to meetings," he confesses. "Then I'd start off flustered and sweating which led to my pitch not going as well as I'd hoped. I'd hide it well and did make sales, but I knew I could do better. I realised that I was pretty good at my job and was worrying for nothing, so I made a conscious decision to change. As I was in the car, I would imagine myself in the meeting being really confident and speaking well. Then, I'd ensure I got there in good time and would spend ten minutes sitting in the car with my eyes closed, just relaxing and listening to soothing music." This had a remarkable effect on Matt's life. Not only did he stop getting stressed for no reason, but his sales figures also went through the roof, and he ended up getting a promotion. "This was a win-win for me," Matt continues. "I was enjoying my job much more and not getting worked up about it, while my increased salary put paid to my money worries too."

Worry can be caused by being overwhelmed, with work or personal issues. The key, then, is to use the strategies in this book to make good use of your time and, therefore, keep on top of your workload. If you are worrying about something, take steps to sort it out, one way or another. That will help you to reduce stress and anxiety which, in turn, will help you to make better use of your time. And one of the best is to use a must-do list (see Chapter Four) to ensure that you finish everything you have to do each day, so you're not worried about things piling up.

You should also put things in perspective. If you start to worry about something, ask yourself, "What is the worst that can happen?" You may be pleasantly surprised by the answer. A lot of worry is about what you think someone else is thinking about you. Well, guess what – there's a good chance that person isn't thinking about you as much as you imagine they are. If you still can't get things out of your mind, talk to someone else – the old adage "A problem shared is a problem halved" is very true, and what seems a big deal to you may be trivial to the person you chat it over with and they will be able to help you put things into perspective.

People don't only worry about what might happen, they also worry about what has happened which, when you think about it, is even sillier. What is done is done, and no amount of worry is going to undo it. We all make mistakes, and we need to learn from them and move on. If you had a silly argument with a partner, messed up at work, or broke a favourite ornament, then fretting over it won't help and may even make things worse. So park that mistake and move swiftly on. Imagine your life's events as like goods passing along a conveyor belt – once they've passed you by, it's onto the next thing. Job interview didn't go well? Move onto the next interview. Date was a disaster? Next date. Blew that tennis serve? Next serve. You may even want to say 'next' to yourself each time you mess up as a way of telling yourself to forget and move on.

As the 19th-century writer Ralph Waldo Emerson said: "Finish each day and be done with it. You have done what you could. Some blunders, losses, and absurdities no doubt crept in; forget them as soon as you can.

Tomorrow is a new day; let today go so you can begin tomorrow well and serenely, with too high a spirit to be encumbered with your old nonsense. Each new day is too dear, with its hopes and invitations, to waste a moment on yesterdays." Wise words with which to finish on.

Quickly…

• Most things you worry about either don't happen or aren't as bad as you expect.

• Worrying wastes time and causes stress.

• When you do worry, think back at a similar scenario and how well that turned out.

• Talk about your worries.

• Don't worry about what has already happened – you can't change the past.

Chapter Twelve
Ultimate freedom

"If you don't build your dream someone will hire you to help build theirs"
　Tony Gaskins

　Up until now, I've suggested lots of small changes that you can choose to incorporate into your current lifestyle, to ensure you make better use of your time and money. This, in turn, gives you more freedom to do what you want, when you want. Some of those tips will work for you while others you may decide aren't right for you. It's your choice, but I guarantee that embracing at least some of the suggestions will improve your life, and you'll have more opportunities to do the things you want to do.

　That may be enough for you, and that's great if so, but what if you want more? What if you want total control over your life so that you can call the shots – combining work and pleasure so that you really can embrace life to the full and be a super-lifesaver?

Sounds good? It is, but you have to be prepared to make massive changes to your lifestyle and it may not be for you. Read on and decide.

Let's cut to the chase here – to have this total freedom you need to give up employment and work for yourself. Getting rid of the 'boss' controlling your life makes a huge difference. However – and it's a big however – you need to find a way of earning a living that maintains your freedom, as Peter found out at his expense. Let's allow him to explain:

"I set up my own little IT company, working from home, and was looking forward to having the freedom to go jogging every morning, popping out for lunch with my wife from time to time, and being there to pick up the kids from school. The reality, though, turned out to be so different. I had a lot of work coming in and I didn't like to turn anything away, as I hated the idea of letting customers down and, if I'm honest, I felt I had to make hay while the sun shone in case all the jobs dried up one day. So I ended up working 15 hours a day, getting incredibly stressed and not enjoying myself. I yearned for the old days when I had a nine to five job that I could walk away from each evening."

A cautionary tale there from Peter. Some self-employed people thrive on hard work and enjoy striving to build up a successful business, and that's fine if it's what you want to do and it's what you love.

The key, though, is to enjoy it and that means doing a job that you're passionate about, and then it won't seem like work – you've cracked it when work and pleasure merge into one wonderful life.

Amy succeeded in doing just this. She was a successful manager in the NHS, making reasonable money and earning the respect of her colleagues. The trouble was, she hated the stress and the politics. "It was awful and, although I knew I'd have a good pension at the end of a career in the NHS, the thought of spending the next 35 years of my life working for a big organisation filled me with dread. I needed to do some serious thinking and make some really big changes to my life."

And that's exactly what Amy did. "I thought about what else I could do. One option, which I nearly took, was to retrain as a teacher. I know I'd have been good at this, as I like children, and the long holidays were attractive, but I was worried I'd be leaving one set of politics and going into another. Also, I'd still have to work set hours and, therefore, would not have the freedom I yearned for."

Amy looked at what she was good at and, crucially, what she was passionate about. "Sailing has always been my love from a young age and I'm an accomplished dinghy sailor and yachtswoman," she explains. "I'd picked up a few RYA qualifications over the years, more for my own satisfaction than anything, and when I was a student I'd worked as a dinghy instructor in Greece during the summer holidays. I had a eureka moment when I realised that I could be a full-time sailing instructor and decided that was exactly what I wanted to spend my life doing. I could combine my passion for sailing with my desire to teach."

An ecstatic Amy handed in her notice and immediately began making plans. "I'm pretty switched on when it comes to business," she says. "I knew that the key to success was to be professional, so I set up a website, put posters up in all the local sailing clubs and spread the word among the sailing community. I also approached some sailing schools and soon picked up some work with them. My first season was remarkably busy, with a mix of teaching groups and individuals, and it's gone from strength to strength since. I'm now also working as a skipper on charter yachts and regularly spend time with clients in the Mediterranean. OK, I'm never going to make millions doing this and, if I'm honest, there are times I'm cold, exhausted and just want to go home and curl up on the sofa, but on the whole, I love my new life and feel incredibly blessed."

Wow, what a story! Amy decided what she wanted to do with her life and made it happen, creating a lifestyle that was infinitely better than being in a job she hated for the best years of her life. She pinpointed her passion and ended up making that her livelihood, thus completely merging leisure and earning a living.

The key is to do this in such a way that you're earning enough money while, at the same time, not being stressed out, otherwise you will begin to hate your passion – and that wouldn't do at all. To ensure this happens you need to plan carefully and maybe play around with different ways of working, which is what Keith did. Keith was a high-flying salesman in the corporate world and earned a lot of money but he wanted a change. "My life wasn't my own," he explains. "I was living and working in London with a hefty mortgage to support and my quality of life wasn't what I wanted."

At the age of 50, then, Keith took action. He sat down with a personal coach and examined his life. "At the time, my hobby was photography and I wondered if I could make a living taking pictures. First, though, I had to make some massive changes, starting with leaving my job and selling the house to get rid of the mortgage. Our kids had grown up so my wife and I didn't need the big house and nor did we want to be in London. We moved to a Yorkshire village where we bought a quaint cottage using the capital from our London house, which meant we were mortgage free. That in itself felt so liberating!"

Keith knew that there were many ways of making money in photography but he bided his time. "In my first year in business, I did an experiment, doing a mixture of commercial and wedding photography. At the end of the year, I found that not only had the wedding photography been more lucrative but, more importantly, it's what I enjoyed the most; it's great helping couples' big days to be extra special. So now that's what I specialise in. Sure, I have to work most Saturdays but that means I get time off in the week to walk in the hills with my wife. I've built an excellent reputation for providing a professional service combined with my unique relaxed images and friendly approach, and I'm currently booked up over a year in advance, earning surprisingly good money. I'm doing what I love and I still have time for other things, which seems a million miles from my old corporate life."

A happy extra benefit of working for yourself is that you should pay less tax, especially if you set up a limited company. You can also become VAT registered which means that you can reclaim VAT on purchases you make through the business. It's worth getting advice from an accountant on what is best for you, but at the end of the day, if you pay less tax, you won't need to work as many hours to bring in enough income to live comfortably.

Another example is Lee, who went from city banker to landscape gardener. "I earned a lot of money in the

City and, over the years, while my colleagues were buying fast cars and champagne, I quietly invested my bonuses with a view to retiring early. However, by the time I hit 40 I'd had enough and wanted to spend time with my young family, so I handed in my notice. I had enough money invested not to have to work full time, so I set up as a landscape gardener, working two or three days a week, doing something I love while being outdoors and keeping fit at the same time."

Another inspiring tale, but what of our friend Pete at the start of the chapter? Did he manage to claw back a balanced life after setting up his own business? "After a year of self-employment, I became quite ill," Pete recalls. "I was suffering from constant fatigue, I lost my appetite and often had incredibly intense headaches. My doctor sent me for various tests yet couldn't pin down what was wrong but, at the back of my mind, I knew it was caused by my lifestyle. It was a wake-up call for me to change yet again, and this time I knew I had to get it right."

Pete stood back from his job and looked at what he liked and didn't like about it. "I guess I'm a bit of a geek because I love working with computers," he grins. "However, I'd been unable to say no to clients who always wanted things done yesterday, and that led to me working too hard, doing jobs I didn't enjoy."

The solution, realised Pete, was just to concentrate on what he enjoyed and to drop the mundane, stressful jobs. "I had two clients who were, to be blunt, a pain in the backside, and the amount of time and hassle they caused weren't matched by the sum of money I made from them. So I politely told them I was changing the nature of my business and was unable to work with them anymore. I didn't drop them in it, though, I recommended a friend who was looking for clients and, happily, he now has a good working relationship with them, so that was a win-win all round. I also stopped helping out friends with their computer problems, as I just ended up doing it as a favour with nothing more than the occasional beer for payment."

Having done this, Pete built up the web design side of his business. "I love creating websites, and my clients like the fact that, rather than just churning out a site, I talk with them and advise them on what they need. So many people say they want a website for their business but don't know what they hope to achieve from the site, which is something I can guide them on. I can work from anywhere, using my laptop, and can often be found at a local coffee shop near the beach – or even on the beach! What's more, it's great to do something creative and get positive feedback from customers, rather than just fixing Windows networking problems."

That said, Pete admits that he still does some of this work. "I have kept a couple of regular IT contracts, which pay well and aren't high maintenance. I also replace broken iPhone screens by appointment, with people bringing their phones to me for an immediate fix rather than having to post their phone off, and that's proved popular.

"All in all, then, I now have a reasonable income but, more importantly, I have a balanced lifestyle. Sure, I still have some stress, but I quite like that, and now I can work when I want to, where I want to. My health is back to normal and I have a great relationship with my family. On a lovely summer's day we'll all go out, and I will catch up with my work in the evenings when it's cooler."

Pete has been particularly smart here in that, rather than relying on one income, he has created streams of income – money coming in from different sources. This is an excellent idea if you work for yourself because when you don't have all your eggs in one basket, if one income drops, you still have the others to prop it up.

You can take this one stage further and aim for automated revenue – money that comes in even when you're not working. Book sales are something you could consider – it's hard to make a full-time living as an author but you can at least create an automated income stream so long as you get a few sales, and online publishing is so easy to do yourself these days. Once you've written your book, you can upload it directly to sites such as Amazon and iBooks, and you get a cut of each sale made. It's how Fifty Shades of Grey started out before it was picked up by a traditional print publisher. OK, maybe you won't come up with anything as fruity (or successful) as that title, but if you have a yearning to write a novel or a non-fiction book (hey, such as this one) then crack on and do it. It may not make you a fortune, but the sense of achievement would make it all worthwhile and it would be one thing ticked off that bucket list.

Maurice did just that, he explains: "I'd always enjoyed reading novels and, one day when I was walking along the local canal towpath, I came up with an idea for a story about a boy living on a narrowboat. I went home, made some notes and started writing. It took me a couple of years on and off, but I got there in the end. First of all, I touted the manuscript to traditional publishers and agents, but soon got disheartened at the lack of response – most didn't even acknowledge my submissions. Then I was told about Amazon's CreateSpace which allows you to self-publish a book. It then goes on to be sold on Amazon, both as an eBook and a printed edition. It took a while for me to get the book formatted and uploaded correctly but it was worth it. I then discovered that publishing was the easy bit – I now had to market the book. A website and Facebook page were the first steps, then I got the word out to friends and family, and it started to snowball. Two years later and I've earned about £5000 from sales, which may not sound a lot but it's paid for a couple of nice holidays, and I've got a lot of satisfaction from the project. I'm now working on a sequel, and my wife's planning the next trip!"

Maurice has created a useful additional income for himself, but imagine if you had several income streams like that – you could reach a stage where you were earning enough money to live on.

People make money from online videos, with YouTube giving them a cut of advertising sales, but you need a huge number of views to get even a modest income from this; while it's a similar situation with affiliate adverts on blogs and other websites. It's doable, though, and some YouTubers and bloggers make an incredible amount of money this way.

Alex is an excellent example of this. At the age of 13, he began making YouTube videos talking about computer games. Now in his late teens, he produces a daily vlog (video blog) chatting about what he's up to each day. This gives him a useful income from YouTube and helps to raise the profile of his film production company. He gets to travel the world, buy loads of hi-tech kit and gets a real buzz out of life. Search 'Marzbar' on YouTube to see for yourself.

For most people, books, videos and blogs are additional income streams – get enough of them and you can make a comfortable living from the combined streams. And if one stream doesn't work out, try something else. You can have a lot of fun doing this, and having a number of incomes can be a lot more satisfying than being stuck in the same boring job for your entire working life.

Indeed, this is something that Ben found out at an early age. After studying music at university, he wanted to continue following his passion and make a living as a musician. "So many people told me it wasn't realistic to have a career in music," Ben says. "In fact, all my friends from uni now have non-musical jobs. They all moan that streaming has killed music – even though they are all happy enough to listen to music via streaming services!" Ben, on the other hand, has taken a more positive approach: "You can't change the march of technology and streaming is here to stay, so there's really no point in complaining about it. I just get on with making a living for myself." Ben is in an indie band which plays local gigs and, yes, is on streaming services from which he receives a small income. "At least streaming gets our music out to people, and helps build our brand." If that sounds like marketing-speak, it's because Ben also looks after the marketing for a local music venue, which puts him in contact with other acts and he gets to see lots of live music for free. In addition, he works as a session musician, which has opened a lot of doors and he's played for some well-known names, both in the studio and on stage. And if that's not enough, Ben is also a guitar teacher. "I have money coming in from various sources, or streams if you like, and if one is a bit slow, I can simply divert my attention to another. It gives me huge variety, I'm doing what I love, I'm in charge of my own life and I am earning enough money for my girlfriend and me to buy our first house together." Not bad for a 25-year-old – he's got a bright future ahead of him, unlike some of his fellow students who, says Ben, are mostly stuck in dead-end jobs they hate, simply because they didn't believe they could make a living from their music.

Liam, meanwhile, was a high-flying investment banker in London but had enough of the big city and the long hours. "I now live in a beach house on the east coast of England and spend my summers cruising around Great Britain and Europe in my motor home." Liam earns money as a currency trader, gambling on the changes between the values of currencies between countries. "It's the toughest thing I've ever done," admits Liam. "The large banks essentially play with little people like me, so I have to second-guess them. I need big bank balances and big balls and I've had some big losses and some big gains. On the whole, I do well enough to make a decent living. Crucially, though, I can trade from anywhere in the world using nothing more than my iPhone. I love the freedom I have now and would never go back to being employed."

If you're reading this wondering what you could do to break the shackles of employment, think about what you are passionate about and look at ways you can make money from that passion. A passion of mine is cars, and when I decided to move away from my career in publishing, I set up a small business selling Porsches which I am happily running today. I also write about cars for magazines and, of course, I've written this book. Because I am doing something that I am enthusiastic about, I enjoy myself and that enthusiasm rubs off on my customers, who like dealing with me. I'm not a salesman by any stretch of the imagination, but I love helping people find the car of their dreams and I am always honest and open, which means buyers trust me enough to buy from me and often go on to recommend me to friends. In turn, that makes my job easier than if I was having to work hard at making sales and hitting targets. In fact, most of the time it doesn't seem like work at all, and I decide when and where I'm going to do it.

If you love playing a particular sport, how about becoming a coach, or set-up an online shop selling clothing or accessories for that sport?

It doesn't have to be a sport; just follow your passion. You could sell musical instruments, old books, clothes or even antiques – the Internet makes it so easy to set up a sales business.

Ricky does just this. A keen photographer, he sells antique and classic cameras and lenses on eBay. "I have a small business unit where I keep my stock," he says. "I'm not an early riser, so my wife and I tend to spend most of the morning in bed, drinking tea and reading. I then head off to work where I have an enjoyable tinker, cleaning and fixing cameras, then I photograph them and upload them to eBay. Each day, I have a good few orders to process, pack and send off, then it's home for a quiet evening. If I don't feel like going to work one day, well, I don't. Once or twice a month I have to travel to buy new stock, usually from house clearances, so my wife and I will make that into an enjoyable day-trip, exploring a new area and having a nice meal out. It's as if we're retired already."

Maybe you've worked in finance in the past, in which case, stocks or currency trading could well be an option – you really need to know what you're doing but if you do, the rewards can be good and, crucially, you can work pretty much anywhere you want, using a laptop or smartphone.

That is the key – to choose work you can do anywhere and at any time, but won't take up too much of your day. That way, you'll have plenty of hours to do the other things you enjoy – the things that would otherwise have been put off until retirement. It should also be work that you are passionate about because then it won't seem like work at all.

So first of all, you need to decide what you are passionate about – something which is easier said than done, and you may find that your passion doesn't fit in with your dream lifestyle. For instance, you may love interior design, but there's no point opening up a home accessories boutique on the local high street if you want the freedom to travel the world. A better option, in that case, would be to sell products online so that you're not tied to shop opening hours.

The problem could be, though, that you decide what you want to do, invest time and money into setting up your dream business and then, a year down the line, you decide it's not actually what you want to do, or worse, it's not making any money. And that's a mistake so many people make when they launch a business. They get carried away with spending money on branding, stationery, premises, and other shiny and exciting things without knowing if it's right for them.

The solution is to run the business as a test project alongside what you're doing at present. Let's say you fancy being a garden designer; there's a fair chance that you'll know friends or family with gardens, so offer to do a couple of designs free of charge. Approach it professionally by chatting with the owner about what they want to achieve, take measurements, and produce a proper professional proposal including drawings, a planting list, costings and so on. You should also tell your guinea pigs what you would usually be charging for the service, so you can get feedback as to whether or not they'd use you for real. Don't be tempted to skimp on the detail because it's 'not a proper job' but put your heart and soul into doing the best you can achieve.

Once you've done a couple of projects for free, you'll now have a small portfolio you can show to clients, so it's time to look for some paid work. At this stage, though, don't be investing a lot in marketing; word of mouth is good so promote your services to family and friends. After six months or so of doing this 'on the side', you should be able to get a feel for whether or not you really enjoy doing the work and also if there is a demand for your service or product.

If there is, then it's time to press the big red button and launch your new venture properly. Again, though, avoid the temptation to spend a lot of money on the traditional trappings of a business. Depending on what you're doing, you may be able to be based at home, thus saving on premises, while fancy office furniture, vehicles and expensive branding can wait until you are more established, if you feel you need them at all. Letterheads and business cards can be ordered online for a reasonable cost, while a website can be set up for not much cost. All you need to do is register a domain name (which will also give you an email address) and then use Wordpress to create a site. In fact, when I started my business, I taught myself how to work with Wordpress and got up and running in a few days. It's not at all difficult and it's good to have control of your own site rather than having to rely on a web designer. In fact, once you've learned to build a website, you could create a stream of income doing them for other people!

I suspect that you're now thinking all this sounds great but, actually, you have a steady, secure job with a good income, a healthy pension plan and other benefits. While you'd love to go out on your own and become self-employed, it would simply be too big a job to give up all that security. That's entirely understandable and it is hard to walk away from a good job and head into the unknown territories of self-employment. It's much easier when you are forced to leave a job, as Julia recalls: "I was working in a senior position at a big recruitment company and, at the time, I was reasonably happy there. Without warning, though, the company was bought out by a competitor and was completely restructured, which meant I was very quickly out of a job.

"It was a big shock at first but I got up, dusted myself down, took a deep breath and automatically started looking around for another job. A couple of opportunities came up but, to be honest, they didn't excite me and, all of a sudden, the idea of working for another large company filled me with dread. I lost all enthusiasm for the job searching and began to drift through my days until I had a phone call from a former colleague. She asked me if I'd be interested in setting up a small boutique recruitment company with her, focussing on a very specific market which she'd highlighted had a need for the services we could offer.

"We met up for a quick preliminary meeting in a pub and ended up chatting for hours, bouncing ideas off each other and getting really excited. Before we knew it, we'd agreed to go into business together and I've not looked back since. The company is doing well but we're determined to keep it small, so that we can offer our clients a personal service and, more importantly, we're not overwhelmed with work. Instead of an office, we both work from home and communicate with each other via email and FaceTime, and meet up once a week in that same pub for lunch. Not having to commute to work saves me hours a day, time which I use to go jogging with the dog every morning. I've also cut my car journeys from 20,000 miles a year to just 4000 miles, so I feel I'm doing my bit for the environment, too."

Julia turned a disaster into something really positive which has enhanced her life, and there are lots of other stories about people being made redundant and then setting up on their own. Of course, there's no guarantee that you'll be forced into a lifestyle change in this way – despite the doom and gloom you hear in the news, most people don't get made redundant.

You, then, have to make a tough decision. Do you continue in your safe, secure job that is eating up your days, months and years, until you retire, or do you take the plunge and leave it to pursue a life of freedom? Or at least, move from a job you hate to one you enjoy, even it means a drop in income. There's nothing wrong with having a change of career – in fact, everyone should have more than one career during their lifetime. I've been a marine electronics engineer, photographer, magazine editor, writer, and I now run a car sales business, and I've really loved the variety over the years.

There's no right answer and I urge you to think long and hard before making a choice either way. If you think you don't have the strength to make a major change in your life, turn to the next chapter but before you do, consider this quote by an American author with the splendid name of Whit Hobbs:

"Success is waking up in the morning, whoever you are, however old or young you are, and bounding out of bed because there's something out there that you love to do, that you believe in, that you're good at – something that's bigger than you are, and you can hardly wait to get at it again today."

"Lack of success is waking up in the morning after hitting the snooze button a bunch of times. Doesn't matter how old or young you are, you feel blah. You slowly get out of bed with a feeling of stress about your day. You may have thoughts going through your mind like, another day another dollar. I have to get out of bed and go to my job. Can't wait for the weekend. I am tired of making someone else's wallet fat".

Quickly…
• For ultimate freedom, you have to give up employment.
• Earn money doing something that allows you to work when and where you want to.
• Do something you are passionate about.
• Streams of income are better than having all your eggs in one basket.
• Being forced to work for yourself is easier than walking away from a steady job.
• Have more than one career.

Save Your Life www.saveyourlife.me

Chapter Thirteen
You can or you can't

"Whether you think you can, or you think you can't, you're right"
  Henry Ford

Now you've got this far through the book, I suspect you're thinking roughly along the lines of one of two schools of thoughts. The first is:

  "Hey, this is amazing. I'm going to follow my dreams and live the life I really want. Hang on a minute while I write my letter of resignation…."

The other response will be something like:

  "I've a family to feed and a mortgage to pay. Sure, I hate my job, but I'm stuck with it until I retire."

Which one fits your reaction? Have a think about it and then look back at Henry Ford's wise words at the start of this chapter. It's not your circumstances, but rather how you react to those circumstances that control your life.

Two men were in hospital together after each losing an arm in road accidents. The nurses and doctors were very sympathetic and handed the men leaflets explaining what benefits were available for disabled people like them.

Fast forward ten years. One of the men is living alone in a council flat. He hasn't worked since his horrible injury, and spends his days watching television, drinking beer and eating far too much. Once very fit and active, he's put on weight, rarely goes outside and has cut himself off from his friends and family. He has been on prescription drugs for depression for many years and likes to grumble about how badly done by he is, and how much the government doesn't support those who can't work.

The other man turned down the offer of benefits and went back to his job as an engineer and spent long hours adapting tools to allow him to work one-handedly rebuilding racing car engines. Today he has his own successful business, a loving family and, in his spare time, he works tirelessly raising money for charity and inspiring other amputees. He never complains about his missing limb and is always smiling and enjoying his life.

In short, then, one man adopted a can't do attitude, while the other adopted a can-do approach to life. While losing a limb is an extreme thing to happen, there are often more common situations in our lives where we choose to go down the can't do route because, well, it seems the easier option. Leave your job and work for yourself? 'No, I can't do that'. Spend six months travelling around Asia? 'No, I can't do that'. Buy that old farmhouse that needs renovating and make it into holiday lets? 'No, I can't do that'. Cook a healthy meal rather than ordering a takeaway? 'No, I can't do that'. Often in life, it's easy just to take the easier option even if, long term, it doesn't get you to where you want to be. Sometimes you have to make an effort to create the life that you want. A life where you can do what you want, when you want.

Robert, on the other hand, was pensioned from the army with health issues. With a young family to support, he was determined to make something of his life, and he and his wife regularly talked about success and wealth. They visited prestige car dealerships and chose the cars they wanted to drive; they got estate agents' details of their dream house; they thought of how they would help make their families' lives better if they had the money to do so. In their minds, they lived the life they wanted right from day one. "I knew I was going to crack it and have a wonderful lifestyle," Robert explains. "Over the years, I tried all sorts of 'get rich quick' schemes, including Forex trading, running a self-help website, being a personal fitness instructor, and even started to train as a manager at a fast-food chain – that was a mistake!"

There were times when Robert's faith in his dream was pushed to the limit. "At one point, I decided to give up and I got a job as a labourer just to make ends meet," he recalls. "However, deep down I still knew that one day I would be rich and free." And that is when it happened: "Someone suggested that I write a book about my time in the army and he introduced me to an agent. Before I knew it, publishing companies were fighting over me and I landed a fantastic deal." Robert's book quickly became a best-seller, and he is now working on a sequel and even a television adaptation. His family is financially secure, and Robert has an exciting future as an author and screenwriter. All because he had a dream and stuck with it, through thick and thin.

Some people, like our friend Robert, have a positive attitude to life and that's great, but what if you're not like that? Just go back to Henry Ford's words – if you say you're not a positive person, you won't be. It also helps to mix with positive people who will encourage you to live your dreams. It's much easier to believe in yourself if other people do. We all know it's important to encourage children by being positive about their actions but it's the same for adults. Take a look at the people you hang out with, at work and socially and ask yourself if any of them have a toxic effect on you. You're looking for the sort of people who are always putting you down, putting themselves down and generally moaning about life. They're the people you need to limit the amount of time you spend with. On the other hand, look for those who live the sort of life you want and are always smiling and positive, and engineer things so that you spend more time with them.

Be warned, though; don't fall into the trap of always wanting more and never being satisfied with your lot, as Bruce found out. He runs a yacht brokerage and spends his days at his beautifully furnished office, overlooking a marina, or onboard lovely sailing and motor yachts. "I gave up a corporate life in London to start my own business and there's no doubt it's a great success," Bruce explains. "However, at first, I wasn't happy as I always wanted more: more money, more time, more success. People would often tell me I was lucky to be doing what I loved but I never actually took their comments seriously. In fact, it was my teenage son, who was working with me during the school holidays, who stopped me in my tracks and finally made me take stock. We were sitting having lunch outside the local harbourside pub just along from my office, and he looked up from his burger and said with a grin: 'Dad, you really are living the dream, aren't you?' Wow! I realised at that moment that he was right, I had ticked all the boxes of my life that I'd wanted when I left London. I have my own business working with boats; I live and work by the sea; I have a wonderful family; a nice home and cars; we get to go on foreign holidays; and I can do what I want, when I want. From that moment on, I start each day being thankful for everything I have in my life and, do you know what, it just keeps getting better and better." Proof that successful people earn money by doing something that they love.

Ok, you may not yet have the same dream lifestyle that Bruce enjoys; but you certainly have the potential to do so, and the first step is to always to be grateful for what you have, rather than moaning about your life and constantly yearning for things to be different. Once you do that, you'll be happier in yourself and your whole mindset will be more positive which, in turn, will help you to adopt that all-important can-do attitude. Remember; don't waste your life waiting for the day that 'everything is all right' because that day will never come. Or, to put it another way; tomorrow never comes. Neither should you compare yourself with others – the grass is always greener on the other side, and you don't know what's going on behind the scenes of that guy who seems to you to be leading an ideal lifestyle.

Don't tell me you've nothing to be grateful for – you have, however bad things may seem. Family, friends, a job (even if it's not your dream one yet), somewhere to live, food to eat, water to drink and – the best gift of all – just being alive.

Dare I add 'having the chance to read this book' to the list of things you can be grateful for? If your answer to that is a resounding 'no' then I guess we have reached the end of our journey together, and I thank you for your time and wish you all the best, and hope you picked up at least one tip. If, on the other hand, you are grateful for this book and the advice within it, then I also thank you for your time and wish you all the best in your new exciting life of freedom and fun. Before you know it, you'll be doing what you want, when you want, and living for 360 years.

If you do decide to take the plunge and leave conventional employment, then you need to take massive action – now. Sitting daydreaming won't get you anywhere at all. Make a list of what you need to do and set a deadline – 90 days is a good timescale to make massive changes to your life. Go for it and be a true lifesaver.

Finally, I leave you with this wonderful quote – which is often wrongly attributed to Mark Twain but was, in fact, first quoted by author H. Jackson Brown – as food for thought:

"Twenty years from now, you will be more disappointed by the things you didn't do than by the

ones you did do. So throw off the bowlines. Sail away from the safe harbour. Catch the trade winds in your sails. Explore. Dream. Discover."

Quickly...
- You can or you can't. It's your choice.

Keep in touch at

www.saveyourlife.me

The End

Appendix 1
Resources

Here are some books, websites and other resources that will encourage you to live your life to the full. Remember to choose audiobooks if possible so you can listen to them while doing other things.

Save Your Life
The website and blog that accompanies this book. Check it regularly for updated advice and news.
saveyourlife.me

4-hour Workweek by Tim Ferris
There are lots of good ideas in this to help you free up time and, ultimately, work just four hours a week.
fourhourworkweek.com

The Secret
Rhonda Byrne's film and books encourage you to be grateful for what you have and to focus on what you want.
thesecret.tv

Living Life the 80/20 Way

Richard Koch's book shows how you can apply the Pareto principle to your life.

richardkoch.net

Zestology

Sky Sports presenter Tony Wrighton's weekly podcast about living life with energy, vitality and motivation has some inspiring guests.

tonywrighton.com

How to Do Everything and Be Happy

Peter Jones (no, not the one from *Dragons' Den*) is another advocate of using diaries and lists, and suggests that you have more than one Boxing Day a year...

peterjonesselfhelpbooks.wordpress.com

Flip it

One of the UK's top self-help authors Michael Heppell encourages you to 'flip' situations to get the best out of them.

michaelheppell.com

Philip Raby Porsche

OK, if I can't blow my own trumpet, then who will? This is my Porsche sales and consultancy company.

philipraby.co.uk

Appendix 2
Who said that?

Each chapter of this book begins with a quote from a famous person, either real or fictional. Here's a bit more about each of them.

Marjorie Pay Hinckley

"The trick is to enjoy life. Don't wish away your days, waiting for better ones ahead."

An American author, who lived from 1911 to 2004. She was married to Gordon B Hinckley, who was high up in the Mormon Church and seen by many as a prophet. Marjorie also had a strong faith, and wrote several books on religion and spirituality.

She also said:
"The only way to get through life is to laugh your way through it. You either have to laugh or cry. I prefer to laugh. Crying gives me a headache."

Basil Fawlty

"Voom! What was that? That was your life, mate. That was quick, do I get another? Sorry mate, that's your lot."

The hapless manager of Fawlty Towers hotel in the 1970s television series of the same name. Played by John Cleese, Basil had strong and traditional views on life, and was often either at odds with, or under the thumb of, his wife, Sybil.

He also said:
"It's what marriage is all about. I know – I read it on the back of a matchbox."

Edmond Blackadder

"I want to be young and wild, and then I want to be middle-aged and rich, and then I want to be old and annoy people by pretending that I'm deaf."

The main character in the 1980s comedy television series, Blackadder. This quote is from Blackadder The Third, set in the Regency period when Edmond was the cunning butler and adviser to the Prince Regent.

He also said:
"You wouldn't recognise a subtle plan if it painted itself purple and danced naked on a harpsichord singing 'subtle plans are here again'."

John Green

"One day, you're 17 and you're planning for someday. And then quietly, without you ever really noticing, someday is today. And then someday is yesterday. And this is your life."

Bestselling author of young adult novels, including *Paper Towns* and *Looking for Alaska*. Green is also a vlogger, actor and film producer.

He also said:
"What is the point of being alive if you don't at least try to do something remarkable?"

Mae West

"You only live once, but if you do it right, once is enough"

An American actress in the early 20th century, Mae West was known for her sexual innuendos which regularly got her into trouble with censors.

She also said:
"When choosing between two evils, I always like to try the one I've never tried before."

Denis Waitley

"Life is inherently risky. There is only one big risk you should avoid at all costs, and that is the risk of doing nothing"

An American motivational speaker and author, best known for his book *The Psychology of Winning.*

He also said:
"Get excited and enthusiastic about your own dream. This excitement is like a forest fire – you can smell it, taste it, and see it from a mile away."

Steve Jobs

"For the past 33 years, I have looked in the mirror every morning and asked myself: 'If today were the last day of my life, would I want to do what I am about to do today?' And whenever the answer has been 'No' for too many days in a row, I know I need to change something."

The co-founder and CEO of Apple, Steve Jobs was a pioneer of home computing and, later, the creator of the iPod and iPhone.

He also said:
"My favourite things in life don't cost any money. It's really clear that the most precious resource we all have is time."

Mark Twain

"The fear of death follows from the fear of life. A man who lives fully is prepared to die at any time"

"I've had a lot of worries in my life, most of which never happened"

Mark Twain was an American writer, best known for the novels *The Adventures of Tom Sawyer* and *Huckleberry Finn*. He said a lot of famous things but not every quote attributed to him was by him!

He also said:
"Always do right. This will gratify some people and astonish the rest."

Hilary Clinton

"I've spent so many years commuting, I kind of prefer a home office."

The wife of ex-US president, Hilary Clinton rose to fame in the 2016 presidential race, when she lost out to Donald Trump.

She also said:
"It is often when night looks darkest, it is often before the fever breaks that one senses the gathering momentum for change, when one feels that

resurrection of hope in the midst of despair and apathy."

John Lennon
"Life is what happens while you are busy making other plans"

As one of the Beatles, John Lennon's songwriting defined popular music, and he went on to have a successful solo career before being killed in 1980.

He also said:
"Reality leaves a lot to the imagination."

John F. Kennedy
"Physical fitness is not only one of the most important keys to a healthy body, it is the basis of dynamic and creative intellectual activity"

The 36th President of the USA, Democrat, Kennedy was assassinated in 1963 and, to this day, remains the country's most popular leader.

He also said:
"Change is the law of life. And those who look only to the past or present are certain to miss the future."

Karl Lagerfeld

"Don't sacrifice yourself too much, because if you sacrifice too much there's nothing else you can give and nobody will care for you"

German fashion designer Lagerfeld became famous for his often daring clothes in the 1960s, and is now well respected in the fashion world.

He also said:
"Sweatpants are a sign of defeat. You lost control of your life so you bought some sweatpants."

Tony Gaskins

"If you don't build your dream someone will hire you to help build theirs"

Gaskins is one of America's most popular motivational speakers. He is also the author of several self-help books aimed at helping women with relationships.

He also said:
"To be content does not mean that you don't desire more, it means you're thankful for what you have and patient for what's to come."

Henry Ford

"Whether you think you can, or you think you can't, you're right"

The founder of the Ford Motor Company, Henry Ford pioneered affordable cars for the masses and embraced mass production.

He also said:
"Failure is simply the opportunity to begin again, this time more intelligently."

Find more inspirational quotes at www.saveyourlife.me

Save Your Life www.saveyourlife.me

About the author

So who is this Philip Raby bloke and what qualifies him to write a book on living life to the full?

Over the years, I've done all sorts of jobs, including a marine electronics engineer (clambering the masts of luxury yachts to fit radars and other navigation equipment), assistant photographer at London advertising studios (big budgets and big lunches), writer and editor for photography magazines (lots of geeky facts and cool equipment), and editor and publisher of car magazines (driving expensive cars fast and sideways).

For some of those jobs, I was employed by someone else, usually a small company, which was fine because I was able to learn how business worked and that put me in good stead for when I set up on my own, running my own businesses. However, when I found myself working for a large publishing company for a while, I realised that life was too short to be under the thumb of someone else. My eureka moment was when a curt memo was sent around the office saying that staff were banned from using the tea and coffee making facilities (a kettle…) until after 10.30 in the mornings. I knew then I had to escape from the rat race and work for myself again.

I handed in my notice and, three months later, had broken free from the prison of employment and I was ready for a new adventure.

And that has led to what I do now. For many years, I had been writing, editing and, finally, publishing Porsche magazines. However, I no longer wanted to be tied down to monthly schedules and, besides, magazines took a big hit with the internet skimming off readers and advertisers. So I turned my back on the industry I'd loved for many years.

I turned my hand to something quite new for me – selling cars. Or, more specifically, Porsches: a subject I know well and am well-known for from my magazine years. It's only a tiny business, which is intentional, as I don't want the commitment of a large company with staff, and I hire in help when and where required. I still write; for a couple of magazines, the occasional book project and for my Porsche blog which, ironically and without trying, has a larger readership than the magazine I used to run.

I sell classic and modern Porsches to people in the UK and around the world, and work on a strict appointment basis so I'm not tied to being at the showroom all the time. People come to see cars on weekdays, evenings and weekends, and I do my best to fit in around them, while still maintaining my freedom. Sometimes I'm at the showroom working, other times I'm in my home office writing, or I may be on the beach or at my sailing club with a laptop, tapping away. If the weather's good, you'll find me cycling or sailing. I still work hard but I'm doing something I love, and I have the flexibility to spend time with family and friends, not to mention doing the things I love to do. My iPhone is always by my side, so I can take phone or email enquiries wherever I am.

Increasingly, I'm meeting and mixing with other people who have also shaken off employment and, like me, are loving the freedom and flexibility of being in control of their days. They are all happy people who love their lives. On the other side of the fence, I know people who are still in nine to five jobs. Some, to be fair, are quite content plodding away, but others are positively miserable about their employment and the restrictions they have placed on them.

I'm not saying my life is perfect but then I suspect I'd be bored if it was. Sure, I have challenges to deal with, times when I wonder when the next month's salary will come from, but I wouldn't swap my life for anyone else's.

Keep in touch at

www.saveyourlife.com

Printed in Great Britain
by Amazon